Praise for *Into the Fire*

"Leaves you gaping in admiration at Medal of Honor winner Dakota Meyer's courage but ultimately sharing in his frustration . . . Dakota Meyer's story of courage shocks even the most jaded and cynical reader." —*National Review*

"*Into the Fire* is a deeply compelling tale of valor and duty. Dakota's storytelling is precise and, for a Medal of Honor recipient, touchingly humble. With deft prose he drops us smack in the middle of one of the most heinous small-unit firefights of the current wars." —ANTHONY SWOFFORD, author of *Jarhead*

"Not a page of *Into the Fire* is wasted. . . . Mr. Meyer is a simple warrior who worked by a simple dialectic: When you shoot, you hit or you miss; and when you fight, you live or you die." —*The Wall Street Journal*

"Superbly reported and compelling . . . [*Into the Fire* gives] voice to a naïve but patriotic farm boy from Kentucky who enlisted in hopes of seeing combat, and then, seeing it, responded with great courage." —*Los Angeles Times*

"[A] breathtaking recitation of one of the most vicious fights of America's time in Afghanistan . . . While most books would concentrate solely on [Meyer's] actions, *Into the Fire* excels by explaining *why* Meyer believes 8 September was the worst day of his life. This is an extraordinary book." —*Marine Corps Gazette*

"Cathartic . . . Combat memoirs don't get any more personal, and Meyer deserves honors for his honesty here just as much as for his experiences in the field." —*Kirkus Reviews*

ALSO BY BING WEST

The Wrong War: Grit, Strategy, and the Way Out of Afghanistan
The Strongest Tribe: War, Politics, and the Endgame in Iraq
No True Glory: A Frontline Account of the Battle for Fallujah
The Village
Small Unit Action in Vietnam
The Pepperdogs

INTO THE FIRE

INTO THE
FIRE

A Firsthand Account
of the Most Extraordinary Battle
in the Afghan War

DAKOTA MEYER
AND BING WEST

Random House Trade Paperbacks · New York

2013 Random House Trade Paperback Edition

Published in the United States by Random House Trade Paperbacks,
an imprint of The Random House Publishing Group,
a division of Random House, Inc., New York.

RANDOM HOUSE TRADE PAPERBACKS and colophon are
registered trademarks of Random House, Inc.

Originally published in hardcover in the United States by Random House,
an imprint of The Random House Publishing Group,
a division of Random House, Inc., in 2012.

Library of Congress Cataloging-in-Publication Data
Meyer, Dakota.
Into the fire : a firsthand account of the most extraordinary battle in the
Afghan War / Dakota Meyer and Bing West.
p.   cm.
ISBN 978-0-8129-8361-6
eBook ISBN 978-0-679-64544-3
1. Meyer, Dakota.   2. Ganjgal, Battle of, Ganjgal, Afghanistan, 2009.
3. Afghan War, 2001– —Personal narratives, American.   I. West, Francis J.
II. Title.
DS371.4123.G36M49 2012
958.104'742—dc23
2012026889

Printed in the United States of America

www.atrandom.com

8   9   7

Title-spread photo: Capt. Jacob Kerr

To Team Monti:

Lt. Michael E. Johnson
Staff Sgt. Aaron M. Kenefick
Corpsman 3rd Class James R. Layton

And to all the men and women who paid the
ultimate sacrifice for our freedom:

Gunnery Sgt. Edwin W. Johnson, Jr.
Staff Sgt. Kenneth W. Westbrook
Mary Kate Moore
Justin Nathaniel Hardin

The battle of Ganjigal resulted in the largest loss of American advisors, the highest number of distinguished awards for valor, and the most controversial investigations for dereliction of duty in the entire Afghanistan war. This is the story of a man who was awarded the Medal of Honor for his bravery in that battle.

Contents

CONTENTS

Maps

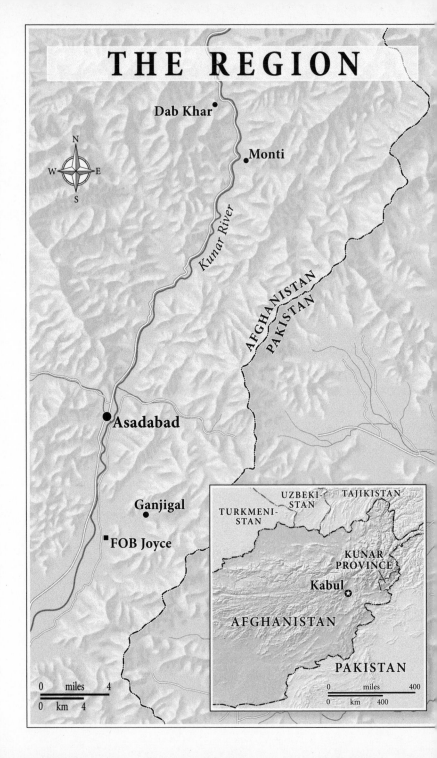

THE REGION

Dab Khar

Monti

Kunar River

AFGHANISTAN

PAKISTAN

Asadabad

Ganjigal

FOB Joyce

0 miles 4
0 km 4

TURKMENI-
STAN

UZBEKI-
STAN

TAJIKISTAN

KUNAR
PROVINCE

Kabul

AFGHANISTAN

PAKISTAN

0 miles 400
0 km 400

INTO THE FIRE

Introduction

ALONG THE AFGHAN-PAKISTAN BORDER

SUMMER 2009

Lt. Mike Johnson, our team leader, leaned his head way back next to my knees and shouted up the turret hole to me:

"We're gonna love it here! Look at those mountains, Meyer! Heavy stuff! Let's go hiking!"

He was yelling over the diesel grind of our Humvee's engine, the deep drumming of our heavy iron suspension, and the clatter of the gun turret, as I cranked the .50-cal back and forth, chasing my suspicions around the landscape from one likely ambush spot to the next. To man the machine gun atop a Humvee, you stand up through a hole in the roof. Your legs are behind the guys in the front seat.

We were roaring through the steep valleys of the Hindu Kush. The Khyber Pass was to the southeast of us—the famed route from the Western world into Pakistan and then India. We were heading north, away from the Khyber, along a river road you wouldn't want to travel without us. Convoys like ours often get rained on by bullets and RPG shells—rocket-propelled grenades. The local drivers of the big civilian trucks will then panic—understandable—and swerve and crash into each other and tip over and catch on fire and block the narrow highway.

The lieutenant and I had become friends during our weeks of training in California's High Sierras. He'd try to beat me to the top of a ridge at the end of each day. Then we'd build a lean-to for the night, boil our ramen rice noodles, and sleep under a zillion stars. You couldn't beat his enthusiasm.

His specialty was communications. Riding now in the Humvee's shotgun seat, he had control of two radios stacked one on top of the other: one for the convoy and one in contact with the command post, which was ten miles back. So he was paying attention to all that and to the risks around us, and, as usual, said something funny to lighten us up, which makes you more alert. Fear slows down your logic circuits, gives you tunnel vision, and triples your heart rate, which isn't helpful in modern combat. A good leader keeps you from getting too scared.

I scanned the bleak ridgelines, the big boulders and small caves, scrawny trees and thorny underbrush, all offering cover for snipers. You look for movement or a reflection. Gone were the stands of soaring green fir trees I'd seen in postcards at the airport. I would soon learn that a common English word that had made it into the Pashto language was *chainsaw*—for decades the mountain tribes had been cutting down their forests and selling the timbers to their rich Pakistani neighbors.

"I'm telling you, Meyer," Johnson said, "I'm going to be a forest ranger and live the good life."

More likely he'd wind up in Silicon Valley, not hidden away in some wilderness, I thought. He was the only married man on our team and had been living on Okinawa with his wife. Truthfully, I couldn't figure out why he had volunteered to be an advisor in the first place. The Afghan Army used Radio Shack–type handheld radios, far below his technical skills. He had mentioned Marine traditions in his family. Being a leader was one of them.

Staff Sgt. Aaron Kenefick was our staff NCO (noncommissioned officer). The way it works is your lieutenant, which in our case was Lt. Johnson, is your leader. Your staff NCO is more the administrator. Staff Sgt. Kenefick was the old man at age thirty, and considered himself the ramrod of our outfit. I had sized him up as your typical platoon sergeant, serious, squared-away, and by-the-book. A true New Yorker, he loved his Yankees and kidded me about my Kentucky accent, which isn't an accent at all but just the way real Americans talk.

Our Navy corpsman was "Doc" Layton, more formally Hospital Man 3rd Class James Layton. As a twenty-two-year-old "boot" (what you're called on your first tour), he kept his medical supplies in meticulous order, according to him anyway, and his mouth shut when he was around Marine veterans. Inside our little team, though, he was laid-back and droll, a classic California surfer dude.

As for me, I was the only grunt on the team, the infantryman and the weapons trainer. I wasn't there to train the other three members of my team, but the Afghan soldiers we were on our way to meet. All four of us were coming in as advisors in our areas of specialty. My desire to see action was a running joke. For my twenty-first birthday, Staff Sgt. Kenefick and Lt. Johnson had presented me with a cake that consisted of a piece of bread with a smoking cigarette on top. The others were looking to do their jobs and return home; I was looking for a fight.

We were rolling alongside the Kunar River now, nearing Combat Outpost Monti, the mountain ranges on each side looking like the black skeletons of two massive dinosaurs. We drove past valley after valley, steep cuts carved into the mountains by thousands of years of rain, earthquakes, and erosion, each one occupied by a small, illiterate tribe.

My town in Kentucky is surrounded by gentle hills, rich in grass and water. Our tractor blades cut easily through the topsoil. Still, we know the grind of farm work; the animals and crops don't take care of themselves. Farming communities work hard, share a bond with the land, and stick together. One long look at those hollows and the stone homes clustered back in the hills told me all I needed to know about the people we were dealing with. It takes plain stubbornness to hack a living out of that flinty earth. If the villagers supported the insurgents, we were in for a long war.

We drove past a few rugged-looking guys with beards and long sticks, beating their sheep off the road. When I waved, they refused to wave back. The tribes, we had learned, lived by the three rules of the Pashtunwali code: courage, hospitality to strangers, and revenge for personal slights. Tough guys. Since the 1930s, the tribes in Kunar had rebelled seven times against the central government. The Russians in the late 1980s never subdued Kunar. In 2001, Osama bin Laden escaped into Pakistan by way of Kunar. A wild place.

"Why's it called Monti?" I called down to Staff Sgt. Kenefick, who was seated just behind my legs.

"Three or four years ago," he called back, "there was a big firefight. Some Army guys were going up a mountain to set up an observation post. They got ambushed."

Aaron scooted up so I could hear him better:

"Monti was the staff sergeant, and he pretty much did a suicide run to get to a wounded private who was stuck in the kill zone. Monti kept getting pushed back, but then he would make another go. On his third try he got hit and didn't make it. But he called in the helicopters before he made his run. Four guys were killed. Monti got the Medal of Honor. That's why they named the place after him."

For the record, Jared Monti, Brian Bradbury, Patrick Lybert, and Heathe Craig were the brave guys who didn't come back from that one.

A half-hour earlier that afternoon we had rolled out of Camp Joyce, a forward operating base about ten miles south of our destination, Combat Outpost Monti.

In eastern Afghanistan in 2009, the U.S. Army provided the conventional battalions and the Marines supplied the advisors to the Afghan Army. Joyce was the headquarters for U.S. Army Battalion 1–32, tasked with preventing enemy infiltration from Pakistan. Joyce was also the headquarters for the Afghan battalion that we were advising.

While our four-man team was to live up at Monti, Lt. Johnson reported to Maj. Kevin Williams down at Joyce. Altogether, there were twenty-one Marines on the embedded training team, ETT 2–8. We were spread out in different numbers among five outposts like Monti. Each outpost was supposed to block the exit from a key valley. Insurgents avoided the posts by taking back trails around them. And since the tribesmen walked twice as fast as any American, you couldn't sneak up on them out on those trails. The outposts, though, did cut down on the heavy supplies the bad guys moved from one point to another.

Before we left Joyce on the convoy to Monti, the local commander of the Afghan Army, Lt. Col. Eshok, greeted us warmly. He had fought against the Soviets and served as a bodyguard for Massoud, the famous warlord who was assassinated by Al Qaeda, two days before their attack on New York. Massoud was the man who was credited with defeating the Russians in Afghanistan. He opposed militant Islam as practiced by the Taliban and Al Qaeda, and organized the Northern Alliance against them. It was interesting to me that Massoud's picture, and not President Hamid Karzai's, hung on Eshok's wall. Eshok had been on good terms with the advisor team we were replacing and had a standard speech.

"Kunar people like Americans," he told each new team of advisors. "You bring money and build roads. We Askars [the Pashto word for soldiers] are your partners. The border police at this base are okay, but not the local police. They set up checkpoints to steal from the farmers."

As we left Joyce, 1st Sgt. Christopher Garza, the top enlisted Marine on the ETT, said whatever supplies we four advisors needed would be on the next convoy north to Monti. However, the Afghan company we'd be working with would try to use us rather than their own supply line. Major Williams was all about pushing the Afghans to get their shit in order. So we shouldn't do the Afghans' work for them. Hold them accountable. That sounded like a good deal to me. Our headquarters down at Joyce would focus on straightening out the screwed-up Afghan logistics, leaving us four up at Monti a free hand to work on tactics and fighting.

We made our trip to Monti without incident.

Located on the remains of an old Afghan combat base, Combat Outpost Monti was typical of what you would see anywhere in Afghanistan: a flat rectangle of dust and gravel enclosed in Hescos and barbed wire. Hescos were square burlap bags as tall and wide as a man, held together by a wire frame and filled with a ton of dirt: inexpensive shields against bullets, RPG rounds, and truck bombers. At the gates and corners of Monti, two- and three-story concrete towers provided protection and some observation for the sentries.

The base was the size of six or seven football fields, one-quarter set aside for the Afghan soldiers and the rest for the Americans of Dog Company from Battalion 1–32. A hundred-man Afghan company lived in several plywood barracks to the south, separated by a line of Hescos and a parking lot from the barracks of one hundred U.S. soldiers. You have trucks and Humvees parked in rows, fuel and water bladders, a mess hall, showers, and plywood bunkhouses. Enough gravel is brought in so you are not always knee-deep in mud during the rainy season. Everything is prefab: the whole place is a beige and dusty Legoland. Lumber comes in quickly on trucks and copters and the defenses are put together before the enemy can decide what to do about it. Bigger bases are called forward operating bases, or FOBs, and they have compact hospitals and larger gyms. The combat outposts, or COPs, like Monti, were little forts on the frontier where you could be a little bit safer than if you were out in the open. The designation COP or FOB was flexible; a base might get bigger or smaller and still keep its original designation.

We four advisors moved into our own bunkhouse in the Afghan section, which you call a hooch—probably a word picked up by soldiers during the Vietnam war. Our little hooch had concrete walls inside. Ropes were nailed along the walls like towel racks to hang some of your stuff. There were little scraps of paper stapled to the wall—sports team posters, family photos, and calendars. There was flickering electric power from the generators, four beds made from wood, four folding canvas chairs, a plywood table, and four lumber T-stands to hold our body armor. There was an always-chattering tactical radio connected to Dog Company's TOC (tactical operations center), located just across the other side of the Hesco barriers that divided the camp.

A Dog Company sergeant and the Marines we were replacing gave us the camp tour. The TOC was an impressive war room, with good views of everything around. There was a screen for watching live video feeds and replays from aircraft and drones circling the Pakistani border a few miles to the east. There were radio and satellite connections to higher headquarters and to the artillery guns just outside. There was a bank of radios for keeping in touch with patrols in the field, and detailed maps were taped on the walls. In a nearby room, they had a radio intercept unit listening to enemy chatter. Those on watch could steer long-range cameras on blimps floating thousands of feet in the sky and tethered at a base several miles to the south.

The problem with the area around Monti was that the terrain was too rough and steep for any kind of vehicle, once you got off the few roads that went along the rivers and not much more than a few hundred yards up the hollows. After that, it was all foot and hoof, which was why Monti was set up astride a main trail between Pakistan and Afghanistan. The mission was to cut down on enemy infiltration from Pakistan and to hold open a fifteen-mile section of road that ran alongside ridgelines so steep you could roll rocks down on passing vehicles.

The soldiers from Dog Company explained that the enemy was a collection of insurgent groups with different names, grievances, and ambitions. They were Taliban with a small "t." Some were allied with Al Qaeda terrorists; others were warlords and smugglers. Some were die-hard Islamist mujahideen or holy warriors, dedicated to killing infidels; others were illiterate teenagers drawn by adventure and male bonding. In a *kahol*, or extended family, if one son joined the Taliban, the chances were that others would follow to fight in the same gang. If the leader was killed, someone from inside the gang, usually a relative, replaced him.

They warned us never to let down our guard. We lived in the shadow of Pakistan, a vast, 1,500-mile-long sanctuary with disciplined guerrilla fighters. We listened to radio intercepts of insurgents taunting us from Pakistani towns ten miles away. We watched video from UAVs (unmanned aerial vehicles) that showed Pakistani trucks driving up to the border and loading munitions onto donkey trains. In the towns, money-changers sat at glass tables, offering Pakistani rupees for the Afghan soldiers' paychecks. Most of the finished goods in the area—clothes, shovels, pots, bicycles—were manufactured in Pakistan. Families, merchants, smugglers, traders, and insurgents walked daily across the border. To the Pashtuns, Pakistan wasn't a country; it was the far side of the mountain where their cousins lived.

"We'll keep the four of you posted if anything big is going on in the sector," said the sergeant who gave us the tour. "There's a radio in your hooch. You let us know whenever you leave the wire on patrol."

He showed us the gym, the showers, the dining hall, and the Internet stations. Wherever you are these days, you can get satellite Internet and make live video calls back home, so there's a lot of that. "So just make yourselves at home here, and use our maintenance guys if you have any vehicle issues. Don't let things go too long, because these roads really eat up the vehicles."

Well, I'm from Kentucky, and even by my high standards this was looking like a very friendly little town. Dog Company made us feel right at home.

Only in the smallest combat outposts do the Coalition and Afghan troops share the same bunk areas. Monti wasn't that small, but the four of us who had just arrived were bunked on the Afghan side because we were there as advisors. That was fine with me. The sooner we settled in, the sooner we'd be outside the wire on combat patrols, which was where I wanted to be.

A few days later, Staff Sgt. Kenefick and I had finished shaving and were walking out of the head at COP Monti when we heard a few loud pops. We stood there, puzzled. Then there was a *whoosh* and a *BANG!* We dove into a nearby bunker, joined by Lt. Johnson and Doc Layton. Staff Sgt. Kenefick and I were wearing T-shirts and were armed with towels. So I sprinted to our hooch, grabbed my gear and a 240 machine gun, and ran back to the bunker.

"Meyer, you didn't bring my gear!" Staff Sgt. Kenefick said.

Okay, I'm the junior man. I run back to the hooch and return with the sergeant's gear. We sit inside the concrete shelter and listen to a few more pops followed by booms.

"I think they're RPGs," I say. "That means they have a direct line of sight on the camp. We should return fire."

"Good idea," Lt. Johnson says. "Go ahead."

Without thinking, I run outside and see that the sentry post is empty. The sentry on guard has ducked into the bunker. I anchor the 240 on the sandbags inside his post and scan a steep hill to the southeast. About six hundred meters away, I spot a lone dushman, RPG slung on his back, scrambling up the hill. (The Afghan soldiers referred to all Taliban as dushmen, meaning thugs and bandits.) He's a ballsy guy. He walked downslope, took three or four shots in the wide open, and is now heading back up the ridge.

I aim the gun. I'm a sniper; shooting is technique. No emotion.

Sometimes you do think about it. That tiny figure in the distance is a human being. He may be a great guy, or he may be one of those animals who will beat his sister to death for having a boyfriend not arranged by the family. You are not there to judge. My only job is to bring him down before he gets to cover.

I fire burst after burst, walking the tracers up the slope. I hit his legs first, then his back. I keep shooting until I'm tearing up a corpse. I rip through two hundred rounds. The sound of the last rounds echoes down the valleys with no return fire. That RPG gunner died alone. No riflemen were providing cover for him. I wondered if he was dumb, or if he had gotten away with it before. I trotted back to the bunker.

"Why didn't you guys bring me more ammo?" I said.

"Sounded like you were doing all right," Staff Sgt. Kenefick said. "We didn't want to interfere with a tactical genius at work."

In the dim light of the bunker, I couldn't see their expressions. But I knew Lt. Johnson, Staff Sgt. Kenefick, and Doc Layton were all grinning.

"That's what you're here for, Meyer," Lt. Johnson said. "You're the sniper. You're our bodyguard."

"Like Kevin Costner," Doc Layton said, drawling out each syllable.

"An *ug*-ly Kevin Costner," Staff Sgt. Kenefick added.

The lieutenant popped out of the bunker and slapped me good-naturedly on the back. "You're our man, Meyer," he laughed. "We all feel safer with you on the job."

I could take the roasting.

I'd put in four years' training for this role. No, more like twenty-one years. My dad thought I was too impatient to develop into a first-class hunter. He hadn't figured on the U.S. Marine Corps providing me with a machine gun and a two-hundred-round belt of ammunition.

That night, I hit my bunk early inside the hooch. It can get a little smelly in there, but an air-conditioning unit kept it cool when the electricity was working. Though I'm no philosopher, I knew the Indus River was somewhere on the other side of these mountains. In the Hindu holy book, there's a story of a warrior who hesitates to attack because his relatives are in the other army. A Hindu god tells him not to hesitate. His role in today's life is to fight fiercely. Let the gods sort out what happens in the next life. I was down with that.

"That was good shooting, cowboy," Lt. Johnson said as we all quieted down in the dark.

"He's not a cowboy, Lieutenant; he's from Kentucky," Staff Sgt. Kenefick corrected.

"I am a cowboy," I said. "I grew up with cows."

"Yeah, but did you ride a horse?" asked Staff Sgt. Kenefick.

"That would make me a horse boy. I rode a cow."

They laughed. But it was the truth. They didn't know anything about life on a farm.

Chapter 1

FINISH THE GAME

"I hope to have God on my side," President Lincoln wrote in 1862, regarding the Union's chances for victory in the Civil War, "but I must have Kentucky."

That independence of spirit that you might call the nation's soul is alive and well in the farming communities of central Kentucky.

My tiny town of Columbia might be considered poor by some standards. We don't look at it like that. We enjoy being on our own, making do with what we scratch out for ourselves. The land is the reason people stay, generation after generation. If you drive through Columbia, you'll see modest homes and trailers on slab foundations, set near the road. Fields stretch out where cattle and horses graze. Nowadays, farming provides only a supplemental income for most families. Commutes of twenty to sixty miles are common to hold down day jobs. But the land keeps people returning to their homes at the end of the workday—this feeling of space that comes with owning the acres outside your back door.

I'm not saying it's always wonderful. My home life growing up was like tumbling inside a washing machine as I shuttled around the middle of Kentucky with my mother. She was never content to stay in one place, or with one man, for too long. She was as smart as she was independent, though, and always landed some job that brought in a little money.

Summers provided stability because my mother let me stay for weeks at Mike Meyer's farm. Mike was briefly married to my mother, and he legally adopted me when I was born. As for my biological father, I had no contact with him. I learned early on that just because you come from the same blood as someone doesn't mean they are family. Big Mike Meyer was my real dad as far as I was concerned.

Big Mike, a University of Kentucky graduate, owned a three-hundred-acre farm in Greensburg. He worked for Southern States, a farmer-owned cooperative, and brought in extra cash by raising beef cows. He lived in a plain house surrounded by open fields, with no curtains on the windows or pictures on the walls. He came home each day, put on his overalls, and tended to chores. Big Mike liked a steady routine, hunting, and the satisfaction of a well-run farm.

His dad, Dwight, owned a bigger farm on the other side of the creek. Dwight had served in the Marines and had later been an engineer. He held himself and others to rigid standards, as if he could see the proper ways of living by looking through his surveyor's scope. He was, and still is, a fair but hard-to-please man. Despite my falling short fairly often, he always seemed to think I was someone worth having in the family. If you can feel that from your family, nothing can touch you.

When asked to describe my nature, Big Mike likes to tell the story of the ATV. Big Mike kept his all-terrain vehicle in the shed next to the house. Consisting of a motor, a seat, and three or four wheels, the ATV is the twentieth-century horse on farms across America. It goes anywhere on a few gallons of gasoline and you don't have to shovel out the stable afterward. It can speed across fields, splash through creeks, and claw up hillsides. Without the ATV, life on a farm would be pure drudgery.

As a four-year-old, I was obsessed with it. I'd perch on the seat for hours, begging Dad to take me for one more ride. Finally, he decided to teach me a lesson.

"Ko," he said, which was my nickname, "I have work to do. No more rides. When you're big enough to start the machine yourself, you can drive it yourself."

Since you had to kick-start it like a balky motorcycle, Dad thought it would be a year or more before I could do that. He'd sit on the stoop after work, smiling as I pushed my little legs down, time and again. This went on for weeks. The angrier I got, the more I tried. The thing would not budge. We are both pretty stubborn.

Big Mike was in the kitchen when he finally heard *chug-chug* and rushed outside to see me smiling brightly. I'd figured out how to climb up on the seat and jump down on the kick lever with all forty pounds of me until that damn ATV started. So he let me take it for a spin.

When I was eight, Dad brought me to his favorite tree stand on a cool October morning before dawn. He was brushing leaves away to climb up into the stand when a deer walked into the open behind him, not fifty feet from us.

"Dad," I whispered, "there's a deer."

He squinted over his shoulder in the thin light.

"If it has horns," he whispered, "shoot it."

I let go with a shotgun. The deer leaped straight up in the air and crashed down on its side without quivering. I had killed an eight-point buck.

When we butchered the carcass, I was so excited that the warm guts and the heavy smell of the blood didn't bother me. In the years after that, hitting moving animals and birds gradually became second nature. Cutting up fresh kills, ugly as that sounds, accustomed me to what I would encounter a decade later on the battlefield.

I had been in grammar school only a few years when my mother called Big Mike to say it seemed best if I stayed with him permanently. One short phone call and my life had changed for the better.

When I was eleven, my school held a contest for the best public speaker in each grade, and Big Mike encouraged me to enter.

I wrote down what I wanted to say, and Dad and I practiced my lines at least ten times a day.

"Slow down when you speak," he said. "Think about your main message and say it clearly."

Each speaker had three minutes. When it was my turn, I talked about Tinker Bell, the Cowboy Cow. We had no horses on our farm, so I picked out this big old cow and petted and talked to her every evening. When she learned to come to my voice, I rewarded her with peaches and Dr Pepper. Eventually, I was riding her to herd the other cows and lasso them. I concluded my speech by declaring that Tinker Bell and I could win any cow race in the county, maybe in the whole state.

My little speech won first prize for the sixth grade. From that tiny victory, I developed a confidence in speaking up that would later exasperate Marine sergeants (and cause me some grief on occasion).

. . .

Each year, Dad gave me responsibility for ever more serious chores. When I was in the seventh grade, Grandfather Dwight—Dad's dad—came by one fall day while I was driving the big tractor, spiking balls of hay. This meant I was constantly shifting in the seat to look down at the steel forks and keep them aligned. Grandfather Dwight lit into me with his booming voice. He thought I'd tip over the tractor and be crushed.

When Dad got home an hour later, one glance told him what was going on with the tractor and me and Grandpa. I was trembling and shaky. Dad put his arm around me and looked at his father.

"He knows what he's doing," he said. "Ko, you go finish moving in hay."

When I was in the eighth grade, we were still growing tobacco on our farm. In summer, when the broad leaves on the tobacco plants reached as tall as a man, you'd hack off the stem and thrust a wooden pole through the leaf. When you'd speared ten stalks—twenty or more pounds—you'd stack the load in the patch for a few days, or toss it onto a trailer to take and hang in the barn.

Mexican itinerant workers came to do the cutting. The pay was ten cents a spear. I asked Dad to hire me. I would work for an hour and then collapse for two. The Mexican workers stayed in the fields ten hours a day, hoisting sixty spears an hour. They were the hardest-working men I've ever seen.

You could wear long-sleeved clothes, gloves, and a mask or kerchief to protect yourself while cutting. I chose not to, so all that tobacco would rub in through my sweat. After work, I'd vomit until I had retched out the nicotine poison. One night I couldn't stop throwing up and Dad rushed me to the hospital. Even after they pumped fluids into me, I was so dehydrated I couldn't pee. The nurses were about to put in a urinary catheter when my dad, laughing at my expression, persuaded them not to. Most small farmers quit raising tobacco after the legal settlements in the late '90s. I often wondered what became of those tough, cheerful Mexican workers.

I did all right in school, especially in math. Dad did not let up on me. When I left the laundry half done one day—I had stayed out too late and, for once, got home after he did—he had tossed the laundry out onto the lawn so I could start over and do it right.

But he didn't do stuff like that often because he didn't need to— I was listening and learning.

Grandfather Dwight helped me with math and geometry as I went further in school. Being an engineer, he showed me that a formula is just like a little machine you needed to figure out.

"It's all simple logic, once you can see it right," he told me. "If you put it together right, it runs. If you don't, it won't." I liked the fact that math was black and white, yes or no, right or wrong, with no bullshit gray zones.

In high school sports, I wanted to be a running back. I was too big to dodge around quickly, though I could smash into the opponents just fine. To improve my agility, I put bales of hay out in the fields and practiced dodging through them.

Coach Mike Griffiths became a third father figure for me. By my sophomore year, I was the starting back in junior varsity. For me, football was a game of high-speed chess—you are looking for holes, thinking a few moves ahead, exploiting weaknesses, and looking for cover. You are zigzagging into the fight or out of it toward the goal.

I dated girls and enjoyed high school life—I tended toward tiny brunettes—but my life was mostly a gladiator school of, by, and for three demanding men—four including myself.

All that testosterone made me a little rough around the edges. I tried to have some sensitivity around sensitive people, but generally, I would rather have punched a guy and gotten punched back. I have a sweet cousin, Jennie, who is my age. We were in the same high school and I said something to her that was a little mean. It wouldn't have been anything if I had said it to her in our own backyard, as she would have just given me a face and thrown something at me. But around her friends, it came off differently. She went home upset.

Her dad, Uncle Mark, drove her over to our house and asked me to look at how upset she was—"Ko, if you don't stand up for your family, you'll never have anything worthwhile in life," he said. Dad was there, too, arms crossed, nodding his agreement. I apologized to her and decided I would have to work on that side of my brain. I would get sensitive.

Dad didn't want me to get carried away with that, however. In about the eighth game of the season, we were playing a team that shut down our passing game. Coach Sneed, one of my favorite coaches, had me run the ball a dozen times in the first quarter, mostly power plays straight ahead into the line. Carry after carry, a pile of big bodies drove me into the dirt. We scored once, with me buried beneath a thousand pounds of sweaty, swearing hulks.

By the next quarter, everyone in the stadium knew what every play was going to be. Grind it out, gain three yards, keep possession, and above all, don't fumble. Time after time, I'd tuck the ball into my chest and slam my ramming arm into three or four speeding refrigerators.

At halftime, after twenty-three carries, I staggered into the locker room, my left elbow so banged up that I couldn't bend it. I sat down in agony. Coach walked over with a bucket of ice, placed my elbow in it, and led the team back on the field for the second half.

A few minutes later, Dad burst into the locker room.

"Get out there and finish the game," he said, and stormed out.

When I walked out to the field a few minutes later, Coach looked at my dad up in the stands and put me back in.

I was driving my four-wheeler out to the end of my road when my cousin Jennie came speeding by. She hit the brakes and backed up, and we chatted. As she left, I told her she needed to slow down. She laughed and said she was always in a hurry. The next day, she crashed fifteen feet from where we had spoken the night before. She was in a coma for a time in Louisville. I would go visit her and, just sitting there and looking at her, I got some work done on the sensitivity thing. I even whispered, "I love you, everything is going to be all right," and she squeezed my hand. It took her a long time and a lot of work, but she has now graduated from college and gotten married. One thing I can say is, the Meyer family is not one for giving up. They don't let you.

That winter, I started in on basketball, practicing like a madman, but I wasn't right for it. After a few games, Coach Curry let me know that I had set a new school record for turnovers. I decided it was my time to go into retirement to help the team.

That kind of jock community was all I knew about, however, so until football started up again, I helped the coach and did some motivation stuff for the team, just to be around my friends and feel useful.

My sensitivity thing was going pretty well, too, until I got into an argument with a girl and she stuck a pair of scissors into my chest. It sounds worse than it was. We were hanging decorations in the gym for a big dance. I made some stupid remark to her—I was actually attracted to her. It sure didn't come off well, as she threw her scissors at me without thinking, and they somehow just stuck in my chest. They didn't go deep, but I had a lot of muscles there that just held the tips, so there they were. People screamed as though I had been murdered, but I just plucked the scissors out and went for some Band-Aids. Since I had started the altercation, I got suspended. Until then, I thought I was doing well on that front, but I had a ways to go.

Dad said I had better get it figured out before I met a girl with a gun.

The school guidance counselor, Ann, was a friend of our family who had known me all my life. When I needed social coaching or some tips on talking to girls without getting stabbed, I'd troop into Ann's office and sprawl on a chair while she explained the basics: be honest and upfront, care about what others are doing and what they care about, don't tease, listen, listen, listen, and take people's emotions and worries seriously. Special reminder: do not make fun of people in public. Write that on your hand.

I was okay talking to guys. If we had disagreements, why, we could just start fighting. I was a typical heavyweight in that department. I'd paw with my left, then plow in with my right, using it like a pile driver, hammering away. Most times, the other guy and I would end up grappling for a headlock while banging away, usually ending up on the ground with torn shirts, scraped elbows, and bruised faces—hoping, by the way, that our friends would please pull us apart. I figured as long as my win/lose ratio was at 50 percent, I was doing okay.

When I was fourteen, my best friend, Mike Staton, tagged me with a roundhouse that knocked me off my feet. A dazzling white light exploded behind my eyes. At the hospital, the doctor confirmed

I had suffered a serious concussion and should take up another hobby. For quite a few days, any sudden move sent an electric shock of pain around my skull.

In my senior year, a football injury ended my dream of playing college ball. I was the stereotypical cocky jock who had fizzled out. True to form, I tested how far I could push the buttons of some of my teachers. I got into the habit of leaving school in my Dodge truck at lunchtime and not returning. Dad didn't know I was screwing up.

Somehow, I got involved helping a teacher, Mrs. Rattliff, who was working with autistic kids at the school. Maybe the way they stayed to themselves made me relate. I asked Mrs. Rattliff if the autistic kids could use any help.

Well, those kids were amazing. They picked up fast on everything. I liked seeing them improve. I enjoyed horsing around with them when lesson time ended. We'd walk down the corridors together, our own little group of happy misfits.

But, in terms of a football scholarship, I was pretty screwed. I was walking through the cafeteria in May of my senior year with no idea where I was headed next. My knee had been stitched up twice and I'd had three concussions. I had one vague scholarship offer from a vague college, but even if I faked my way through the entry physical, I knew my knee wouldn't last another season. I was washed up as an athlete and I hadn't developed strong study habits—I was bored by academics. I sure didn't want to waste Dad's hard-earned money drinking beer and cutting classes at some college.

I walked by a table with brightly colored brochures set up opposite the serving line. A rugged-looking sergeant with a crew cut stood behind the table. He was wearing dress blues. He looked like he owned the state of Kentucky.

"Have you been in combat?" I asked.

"Yes, sir, that's what Marines mostly do," he said. "Fallujah, Iraq. It was a shit hole when we got there and worse when we left."

My granddad didn't talk much about the Marines, but he was proud of his service. I knew they were tough.

"Yes, boot camp is rough and not everyone makes it through," the sergeant told me. "The pay isn't bad, seeing as we pay your room and board and ammunition."

I asked him some questions. No, he didn't like the M4 carbine—not enough stopping power. He preferred the 7.62.

"So do I," I said. "The .308 can put down a big buck."

My obvious reference to hunting fell on deaf ears. He wasn't impressed with shooting something that couldn't shoot back.

I felt I was taking an interview and failing. The sergeant was no more talkative than I was.

"So what are you planning to do?" he concluded, signaling he had given me enough of his time.

"I don't know. Probably go to school. Play some college ball."

He shifted around the brochures.

"Yes, you do that," he said, "because you'd never make it as a Marine."

I knew he was baiting me. He straightened his stack of brochures, letting the fishing line play out. Right, I couldn't ride that big ATV. No sense in even trying. I actually left the cafeteria before turning around and walking back to his table, his silver hook in my cheek.

"You have the papers to sign up?"

"You're seventeen. Your father has to sign. You're not grown up yet."

"If I'm going to be in the Marines, I want to be in the infantry. I want to fight, not sit behind a desk."

In 2006, our country was in two wars. We had been attacked on

9/11. I was thirteen when I watched on television as the Twin Towers caved in. I was more than willing to fight the bastards who had murdered three thousand Americans.

"I'll guarantee you a tryout at boot camp," the sergeant said. "If you make it through, you can become a grunt."

An hour later, he followed me out to our farm, where we sat around the kitchen table and he told me about the fighting in Fallujah.

"A lot of shots at five hundred meters," he said, "straight down the streets."

"I could hit at that range," I said.

"Uh-huh."

I don't know whether he believed me or not. We sat without saying much more until Dad walked in after work. He looked at the two of us.

"Ko," he said, "what have you done now?"

The three of us talked for the next hour. There was no hard sell. The recruiting sergeant and my father left the decision up to me.

"I don't want to go to college, Dad," I said. "And I don't want to stay here herding cows. I want something better."

"Well, Ko," he said, "I don't disagree with your choice."

Chapter 2

THE MARINE YEARS

The good-byes were somber when I left for boot camp. Dad was okay, but not really happy to see me go. Granddad told me I'd do fine if I didn't piss off any of the sergeants. My guidance counselor, Ann, was somber. Her husband, Toby, a state trooper, had worked on our farm when I was about eight. Ten years my senior, he taught me how to spear tobacco and stalk turkeys. Ann and Toby had spoken up over the years whenever I needed it. None of my family came right out and said it, but my desire to be a Marine grunt in combat naturally did concern them. I'm sure there's not one family in America that doesn't have worries when a son or daughter goes off to war.

I sat among twenty other quiet recruits for the fourteen-hour bus trip from Louisville. At three in the morning, the bus started along the causeway that crosses the swamps around Parris Island, South Carolina. At the front gate, a sergeant boarded the bus.

"Put your heads between your legs!" he yelled. "Don't move or blink."

Then the bus door closed and we continued on for what seemed like the longest drive ever.

We came to a stop and the door opened. I heard the slow stomp of footsteps.

"Get your asses out of those seats!" a drill instructor boomed at us. "Outside! Keep your mouths shut and follow the yellow footsteps."

So it began: close haircuts to strip away your old identity, exercises to prove you're not half as strong as you figured, simple tasks that show you are mentally weak, drill instructors who mock your attempts to look tough. It's right out of the movies, but it never stops.

We were handed a blanket and two sheets and told to make our bunks and then stand against the wall.

"Time's up!" our drill instructor, Sgt. Brady, yelled a few minutes later.

About half the forty bunks in our squad bay were made in time.

"Rip 'em off! Start again!"

Thirty bunks made. Brady would walk through and inspect a neatly made bunk. He'd nod, move to another bunk. Not good enough.

"Rip 'em off!"

Eventually, we figured out that the exercise was about helping each other: one fails, everyone fails.

Not all the weakest links would survive, however, and the idea of returning to Kentucky in disgrace terrified me.

I'd crawl under my blanket at night, turn on my flashlight, and write letters to Dad. I missed my life back in Kentucky.

The second month is the turnaround, when they build you back up. Sgt. Brady made me a squad leader, meaning he yelled at me for the mistakes of ten other recruits. That was all right; he had his job, and I had mine.

The third month of boot camp was actually fun. We spent time on the rifle range, which I enjoyed, and Sgt. Brady took to harassing me for the sheer glee of it.

On family day, the day before graduation, Dad introduced himself to Sgt. Brady.

"Looks like you've taken a few pounds off, Dakota," Dad said. Then, turning to Brady, he said, "He seems in fighting shape. You don't have an easy job. Sergeant, I'd be pleased to buy you dinner."

Graduation Day was impressive: a band with the deep drums and sharp bugles, the pennants waving proudly, four hundred new Marines marching in step, colonels saluting generals, and friends and family applauding and waving.

I spent the next two months in the SOI (School of Infantry). Only 15 percent of the Marine Corps (and the Army) are in the infantry. In today's military, there are more combat pilots than infantry squad leaders.

At SOI, a hundred fundamental tactics were hammered into me, such as laying down a base of fire before maneuvering, understanding enfilade and grazing fires (an enfilade position lets you fire down a long line of the enemy, like you're at the end of their trench; grazing fire is just sweeping the ground with heavy fire a foot or two up over the wide terrain of the enemy's position), and learning how to read terrain and translate squiggly lines on a map into your position on the ground.

A Marine squad is comprised of three four-man fire teams. Everything you do as a rifleman revolves around that four-man team. One man carries a weapon more powerful than those of the others, but that's a minor point. In the field, you don't do anything without those three other guys. You don't shit, sleep, eat, or move without the other three knowing about it.

A Marine squad with those three fire teams is like a boxer with three arms. One arm jabs with bursts of fire to keep the opponent off-balance while another arm loops around with a left hook, with the third arm ready to follow up wherever there's an opening. If one arm is wounded, the other two can keep fighting. Fire to pin down the enemy; maneuver to finish him off: fire, maneuver, fire, maneuver.

Five months after joining up, I finally joined a real Marine rifle battalion: the 3rd Marine Regiment in Hawaii. On the day before Thanksgiving, 2006, I lugged my seabag up the steps of a dilapidated barracks in paradise. By way of greeting, some old salts on the second deck pelted me with beer bottles and shouts of "boot!"

I was assigned to a four-man fire team led by Lance Cpl. Daniel Kreitzer, age thirty, who had enlisted in response to the Twin Towers attack. He would lead us to Iraq, where he had already served.

We three team members lived in one dingy room, while Kreitzer lived down the hall with other team leaders. He let us know we were nothing until we proved ourselves in Iraq.

Kreitzer loathed the improvised explosive device, or IED— a primitive land mine that ripped your legs off. You hear about the big ones, designed to take out a Humvee, but they also made smaller IEDs to kill a soldier just walking down a street. The insurgents would bury a plastic jug filled with homemade explosives, insert a long wire, hide nearby, and touch the wire to a flashlight battery as you walked by. On his prior tour, Kreitzer had picked up the blown-up body of one of his buddies.

We spent a lot of time moving fast in seventy pounds of armor and gear, losing a gallon of sweat in the high humidity. No matter how tired we were, we never moved without one team member watching over the other three, checking for anything out of the ordinary. We learned how to skirt around trash piles, avoid freshly turned dirt, and take each step knowing that if you relax, you're dead—or, even worse, your friends are.

In February of 2007, four months into Hawaii, I saw a bulletin announcing openings in the sniper platoon. In the barracks, I had heard that the firefights in Iraq's Anbar Province—the Marine area—had slackened. The war was rapidly winding down.

I was going to miss the show.

If I could qualify as a sniper, however, it would improve my odds of getting into the fight. Sniper school isn't about perching up in a palm tree and taking out some guy down the way, it's about tactics and weapons. I wanted to learn more, but leaving the fire team wasn't easy.

Kreitzer wasn't happy that I wanted to try out.

"Meyer," he said, "I spend four months shaping you up, and you repay me by leaving the team? That sucks."

My instructor was Staff Sgt. Mike Skinta for the next eighty exhausting days, starting with learning heightened powers of observation. We had to map terrain and pick out hidden objects in the distance with our spotting scopes. The goal was to make us see needles in haystacks, move quietly and invisibly, and estimate long distances down to a few feet.

We spent weeks shooting; hitting difficult targets became second nature. You have to squeeze the trigger so evenly that you don't anticipate the recoil and throw the shot off.

. . .

Sniper school provided the finest training of my career. The Marine Corps emphasizes marksmanship. Every Marine is a rifleman. It makes no difference what rank you are or how sophisticated your job is. Marine Gen. Jim Jones was the Supreme Allied Commander in Europe and served as President Obama's first national security advisor. Even in those prestigious top jobs, he still signed his emails as "Rifleman."

The Marines were generally acknowledged as having the finest sniper training program. In the Corps, if you qualified as a sniper, you received a special "military occupational specialty"—0317. I didn't know if I could achieve that distinction, though. The attrition rate in sniper school was close to 50 percent.

Outside military circles, the word *sniper* holds a mystique. People ask only one question of a sniper: "How many men have you killed?"

On one level, that sounds reasonable. It's like asking a baseball player how many home runs he has hit. The Finnish sniper Simo Häyhä held the world record. During the winter war of 1939–40, he killed more than five hundred Russian soldiers. He was called "The White Death" because his white camouflage uniform blended into the snow. Other snipers, too, had astonishing numbers of kills. In World War I, a platoon of South Africans, recruited from big game hunters, averaged 125 kills per man. In Vietnam, Marine Sgt. Carlos Hathcock killed ninety-three of the enemy. In Iraq, Chris Kyle, a SEAL, recorded 160 kills.

I quickly learned, though, that asking in sniper school about kills was the surest way to anger an instructor. Nine times out of ten, the poor bastard seen in a sniper's scope never knew he was about to die. Taking the shot that killed a man was only one small aspect of being a sniper.

"We don't judge each other based on the number of kills," Staff

Sgt. Skinta, my instructor, told me. "How many enemy you shoot depends on luck—on whether you're assigned to a hot or a cold battlefield. The most respected snipers are those who plan the most thorough mission."

We beginners learned over the next eighty days what the word *thorough* meant. The instruction started with the basic power of observation, studying terrain and movement at near and far distances, then providing sketches of the land, its key features and its occupants. It was Kim's Game on steroids—you stare at a complex set of objects for a minute and then from memory produce an accurate sketch. In sniper school, we had to pick out ten hidden objects with our M49 spotting scopes.

Next came complex field navigation, where you are dumped out at night in the middle of nowhere with a map, a compass, and a grid destination, with instructors driving the roads trying to catch you. Good luck puzzling out where you are and selecting a route that will get you to the end point in time.

After that, we practiced estimating (without instruments) distances up to a mile. Out to half a mile, we had to be able to judge within one hundred meters the distance to a man standing erect. Our academics consisted of ballistic physics, target assessment, artillery and mortar calls for fire, intelligence assessment, weapon systems, and mission planning.

With over a hundred sniper teams in the Marine Corps, standard sets of weapons were required. You couldn't have each sniper choosing his personal rifle and cartridge. I enjoyed reading shooting magazines, but most of that gear was for wealthy civilians, not us corporals. Small differences in machine precision counted for far less than individual discipline.

The M40-A3 was our 16.5-pound sniper rifle, equipped with an adjustable cheek rest, a heavy twenty-four-inch barrel, and a bipod stand. The 7.62-millimeter (.308) rifle, based on the Remington 700 short action, fired the M118LR 7.62x51 HPBT military-only cartridge that retained supersonic speed out to nine hundred meters. In addition, we used the standard infantry M4 5.56-millimeter rifle and the monster M107 Barrett .50-caliber.

Our instructors talked about targets they had hit only as a way of illustrating a technique or a lesson. Skinta told of one encounter that had an ironic twist. On one of his tours in Iraq, he was on a patrol hunting for an enemy sniper. At dusk on the third day, the patrol moved to an abandoned water purification building to get some rest. Skinta was on the second floor when the outside wall was peppered by an RPK (machine gun), followed by a few high-caliber rifle shots. Through the scope, his spotter saw a sniper nine hundred meters away. He was shooting with a Russian 7.62 Mosin-Nagant rifle that had a superb pedigree among snipers.

Skinta's first shot was so low that it kicked up dirt in front of the enemy sniper. Yet the sniper didn't bother to duck, probably thinking it was a stray round from the standard Marine 5.56-millimeter M4. Skinta's next shot hit the man in the chest. He died because he didn't realize an American sniper was shooting at him. (For your information: In three combat tours, Skinta tallied over thirty kills. I learned that only by talking with a corporal who worked in administration, five years after I first met Skinta.)

The hardest task for me was the close-in stalk against an alert prey: A truck is parked in the middle of a field, guarded by two instructors with binoculars. You make a ghillie suit from burlap and twigs and grasses at all angles. A man standing up looks like a mass of seaweed.

Lying down, that same man blends into the ground. The test required each of us to sneak a thousand meters across the field, take two shots at targets, and get close enough to copy down the letters stenciled on the side of the truck, all without being seen.

Trying to get that right took me a week of training on my stomach, moving with the ants among stalks of grass and brambles. I learned to observe the enemy by "burning through"—staring intently until you can see through the blades of grass without raising your head an inch. When exam day came, I inched undetected across the thousand meters and simulated my kill shots. That wasn't bad for a guy built like a refrigerator.

We were told that as a sniper, you never let anyone else, regardless of rank, make off-the-cuff changes to your plan. You plan the mission, and you execute it. You're in charge of your team. The goal is to know every aspect of your job so well that you have complete confidence.

Many of the missions we practiced were counter-IED. We spent hours learning how to stake out long stretches of road, waiting for someone to come along with a shovel and a sack of explosives. Skinta told us about a sniper team in over-watch in a half-constructed building in Ramadi in 2004. It was a warm, dull day and after several hours, they dozed off and never awakened. Insurgents sneaked up and shot all four Marines in the head. They left with the high-powered M48-A3 and its excellent Schmidt & Bender scope. Over the course of the next year, they allegedly killed two more Americans before a Marine sniper took them out and recovered the rifle. Skinta hammered home his message: know every aspect of your job, and never, never let down your guard. If you slack off or take things for granted, you die.

Shooting another human being was a math problem. You were either right or wrong, with no subjective in-between decided by someone else. I liked problems that were black or white, life or death. Before taking a shot at a target one thousand meters away, you had to calculate the effects of the light air at altitude, wind, humidity, angle of fire, cartridge velocity, and gravity. You had to align the target, the background, the terrain, the weather, the noise, and the weapon. You had to work in concert with others. At the same time, the target enemy was figuring out how to kill you. Combat was zero-sum decision-making played for the highest stakes, live or die.

My final test was conducted at one thousand yards with the M40-A3. You get two tries. If you hit the man-sized iron target half a mile away, you qualify. My first shot missed. The school's best spotter then gave me the data for wind and elevation. I squeezed off my last bullet. We all heard the distant ping of a good hit.

Thirty-one of us began the eleven-week course; thirteen graduated. Skinta gave us a short talk about that.

"I took no pleasure in washing out most of the class," Skinta said. "I can teach anybody to shoot. I can't teach personal discipline. The test of a sniper is his ability to convince a commander that every step in a mission has been thought through. A sniper is all about maturity."

When we began the course, the instructors called us PIGs, or professionally instructed gunmen. At graduation, each of us received a neck chain with a single 7.62 bullet in a clasp. It was called the HOG tooth, or hunter of gunmen. I was now officially designated as an 0317—a sniper.

On my chest I had inscribed a tattoo in Latin: *Vestri nex est meus vita,* or "your death is my life." My sniper instructor suggested I inscribe the Latin rather than the English translation; otherwise, people would think I was a lunatic. To me, the quote meant that I viewed the act of shooting in black-and-white terms. You either succeeded by hitting the target, or you failed and it's his turn.

After nineteen months in the Corps, I was beginning to put it together. I knew that having a combat action ribbon wasn't what made a good Marine. Instead, it was confidence based on good planning and execution, doing what was right time after time. I had learned from those who did it right, the Bradys, Kreitzers, and Skintas.

In July of 2007 our battalion assumed patrol duties in Kharma, sixty miles west of Baghdad. Nicknamed "Bad Karma," the dingy town consisted of a few dozen narrow, dirty cobblestone streets lined with cramped concrete apartment buildings. A large mosque with a bombed-out minaret had been used by insurgents as a rest stop during the highly publicized battles for the nearby city of Fallujah. In the three years since then, the Marines had employed constant patrolling to grind down the local insurgent gangs. The town was so small that sooner or later, informants pointed out first one terrorist cell, then another.

When we arrived, we were hit occasionally by a few mortar shells from the diehards. Rumor had it they had only one tube. Four or five guys would drive to an open field, hop out, point the tube in the direction of our main compound, pop a few shells down the tube, and drive away.

We couldn't detect a pattern or locate the source. We conducted little visits where a squad or a team of snipers would walk unannounced into a compound after dark, herd the startled family into one room, set up observation posts on the roof, sometimes staying for two days and sometimes leaving the next morning. We were hoping sooner or later to cross paths with the mortar team.

With each compound separated only by a wall from the next, sounds carried clearly down the streets at night. If you weren't careful, soon the whole neighborhood knew that strangers were about. Once, at two in the morning, we sneaked over a back wall into a large courtyard. It was a hot night, and the family was sleeping outdoors. As we shook the owner awake and signaled him to be quiet, I saw a man next door staring at us in amazement. I gestured for him not to speak. That didn't work. Inside a minute, his whole family was awake. So I shooed them into the courtyard next door.

"Meyer, what the hell are you doing?" my startled teammates asked.

The two families together made enough noise to wake up the family on the other side. Again, we herded a wary husband, an irate wife, and sleepy kids into the courtyard. Now we'd collected twenty-three Iraqi civilians, who were highly pissed at being awakened and prodded like sheep from one place to another. So, we apologized and walked back to base the next night, muttering at each other.

On night patrol, you couldn't lie down anywhere in the fields without being bitten by sand fleas. One day I was stung sharply on my right hand. Over the next several days the swelling increased and my hand felt like it was burning off. It was a deep red, with other red streaks running up my forearm. My platoon sergeant brought me to the battalion doctor, who took one look and drove me to a hospital. I had been bitten not by a sand flea but by a recluse spider and now had a severe staph infection.

They operated twice in the next two days to save my hand. I was then evacuated to Hawaii. Two years of training for this?

For two weeks I couldn't feel or move my fingers. The doctors recommended a gradual course of physical therapy over six months. I went enough times to understand the principle: exercise the fingers until sufficient pain kicked in to stop the treatment until the next day. I decided to replace the in-clinic daily visit with my own twice-a-day schedule. At first, I could only pull the fingers open like a pair of rusty pliers, with each creak bringing on a wave of fresh pain. So I started drinking Kentucky bourbon. I had nothing to do but drink and bend my fingers. I was knocking back a bottle to a bottle and a half a day, twelve thousand miles away from my platoon in Iraq and six thousand miles from where the bourbon came.

The doctors told me to go home for a week in October. I called Justin Hardin, who had played tight end on our high school team and was my solid, down-to-earth buddy—the calm one in our duo—and told him I was coming. He said we'd be sure to go to a football game or two and hit up a few parties. I was excited. Maybe a girl or two would remember me—maybe even Nikki. The doctors were right: just thinking about getting out of the barracks, hanging out where I knew everyone, made me smile.

That didn't work out. Justin was killed in a car crash about three hours after we made our plans over the phone. His car slipped off a rain-slick road and hit a tree.

I was looking forward to going home for Christmas, hoping for some fun, but while home another old friend, Mary Kate Moore, smashed her car and she was gone, too, just after I had seen her pass on the road. I was hoping it wasn't me that was such a good luck charm for my friends. When I was in high school, I had signed up for the track team, doing some sprinting and pole-vaulting, just to jog around the track with Mary Kate. She was a little bitty, peppy thing, and I had a real crush on her back then. Unbelievable. I never liked Christmas much anyway.

In the early winter of 2008, my battalion had returned from Iraq and I was back with them. My platoon sergeant, Gunnery Sgt. Hector Soto-Rodriguez, watched me for a few weeks and then laid down the law:

"Knock off the drinking, Meyer," he said. "You're a sniper, not a screw-off. It's time for you to step up and be a leader."

He put me in charge of a team and challenged me to build us into a top-notch fighting unit. I had a job to do that mercifully took up all my time.

Gunny Soto-Rodriguez sent me to the marksmanship coach course. After shooting hundreds of rounds, I could hit practically anything with a pistol or rifle. From there, I was sent to the mountain warfare center in Bridgeport, California, for the high-altitude sniper course. The center is located atop the Sierra Nevada range, 150 miles east of San Francisco. The spring scenery was stunning and the instructors were veritable mountain men. During the winter, the Marines up there survive in snow caves. In the summer, they scale rock faces at ten thousand feet.

On one exercise, five of us were sent into the wilds with a map and blanks in our rifles to stalk and simulate killing a guerrilla leader. The instructors gave us a can of mace in case we crossed a bear. To avoid enemy patrols, we dug hide sites to sleep in during the day and moved at night through snow-capped passes. The second day, we came across some bear scat.

During the third night, we were walking silently on pine needles through a moonlit forest—it's beautiful up there—when the point man thrust up his right hand. We froze and looked every which way. There in the soft earth next to us were enormous paw prints. Not one of us breathed for the next five minutes. It was so quiet you could hear the moon moving overhead. Suddenly our point man leapt up and ran back to us, his hand clenched like a claw.

Bear!

We froze, looking at the shaggy, crouched monster about to tear us apart. I glanced around and concluded I'd never have time to climb the nearest tree, plus bears climb trees as well and are a lot better than I am at it. We waited like mice for the bear to choose its first victim. After about fifteen seconds, we realized we were looking at a moss-covered stump.

The next day, we found the guerrilla camp and took one shot— a bull's-eye.

When I rejoined my battalion in Hawaii in mid-2008, I was put in charge of my own six-man sniper team. We were tight. When others were around, my team called me Corporal and came to parade rest to report. When we were alone, I told them not to do any of that stuff. We were like the Army Special Forces. We knew our jobs and were relaxed with each other, using first names.

While my battalion was set to go back to Iraq, I figured they would be in a backbench situation. By late 2008, the American battalions in Iraq had pulled back to remote bases. They were no longer conducting combat patrols.

When headquarters asked for volunteers to serve as advisors in Afghanistan, I signed up. I knew that would mean action.

"The Afghans won't have your back, Corporal," my platoon commander warned me. Sergeants who had served in both countries told me the Afghan soldiers were worse than the Iraqis. They called the Afghans pogues, a slang term meaning unreliable and undisciplined.

Just the same, I was looking forward to the adventure. As a sniper with mountain training behind me, I was confident I could handle whatever came my way.

I flew to Okinawa, where I joined an advisor team. In Marine language, that's Embedded Training Team 2–8. Four of the other nineteen team members on ETT 2–8 were infantrymen, and I was the only sniper. Because the infantry battalions were committed to Iraq, most advisors were non-infantry Marines stationed on Okinawa. Since World War II, the Marines had maintained a base on the Japanese island, a thousand miles south of Tokyo.

I flew to Okinawa, where our ETT spent a month concentrating on the basics of fire and maneuver. We didn't know each other and I wasn't impressed with our makeshift workup. We would soon be advising a veteran Afghan battalion fighting in the mountains of eastern Afghanistan, but we didn't follow a serious program of instruction for going to war.

From Okinawa, we flew to the mountain warfare camp in California's High Sierras to acclimate. Since I knew the terrain from my previous deployment at the sniper course, I was usually placed at point on the patrols. During the day the instructors would harass us, shooting blanks from a distant hillside or a thickly wooded draw, and then withdrawing before we could engage them. That was solid training, exactly what was needed to simulate what we would encounter in the mountains of Afghanistan.

In the evening, though, we bedded down without security, as if every combat patrol ended at sundown. We set up lean-tos, spread out pine branches as mattresses, took off our boots, boiled our favorite noodles over bright campfires, and went comfortably asleep under the stars. All we lacked were marshmallows.

I couldn't restrain myself from bitching. My previous sergeants would have kicked my ass down the mountain for camping out Boy Scout style.

Second Lt. Ademola Fabayo, a New Yorker whose parents immigrated from Nigeria, was the operations officer on our ETT, although he did not have infantry training. My focus upon tactics exasperated him.

"We're not going there to fight, Meyer," he said. "Our job is to train the Afghans. They do the fighting, not us."

Back then, and even today, I didn't understand how we could train Afghans in a combat zone while avoiding the fight. There was a huge problem with that theory. In our field exercises, the enemy were American role players with fake bullets; in Afghanistan, the enemy were genuine Taliban fighters. Things came to a head on the last patrol. Everyone was tired as we came down the hill, heading toward warm showers and decent food. The patrol leader left four stragglers on the hillside to wander in by themselves. As we were putting away our weapons, I complained about the haphazard ending. For three years in the infantry, it had been pounded into me to be precise and disciplined. No slack, no shortcuts.

First Sgt. Christopher Garza, the team's senior enlisted man, was a strict but fair man. In retrospect, things might have turned out differently if I had used diplomacy, appealed to his human side, recited my Tinker Bell speech, and got him to smile. Instead, I charged straight ahead and blurted out what I believed.

"We need a debrief to correct our errors, First Sergeant," I said.

"Damn it, Meyer," Garza yelled back. "I'm tired of your negative attitude."

Uh-oh. It was too late for Tinker Bell.

"I've had it with you!" he screamed in front of the team. "Load up your gear and get down to the flight line. You'll sleep on the runway tonight and stay away from us. You're off the team."

A few hours later, Garza calmed down and let me stay on the team. We didn't resolve our fundamental difference. I was still confused. Were we to act as garrison instructors or combat advisors? Either way, we were on our way to Afghanistan.

Chapter 3

MONTI

When we arrived in Afghanistan in the summer of 2009, it was 1st Sgt. Garza who assigned me to Lt. Mike Johnson's four-man team at Monti, ten miles north of Joyce. That way, headquarters didn't have to put up with me on a daily basis, and I'd get all the action I wanted.

Lt. Johnson assigned each of us a specific job. He took on the tasks of improving the leadership procedures of the Afghan officers and coordinating our activities with those of Dog Company. He was the perfect guy for that job—sunny and smiling, with an easy laugh, but completely professional, with the highest standards. I had climbed mountains with him in California, of course, and I knew he was as strong physically as he was mentally. On that first trip up to Monti, when he was saying the mountains looked good for hiking, I knew he could probably give those mountain goat dushmen a run for their money to the top of the ridge if he wanted to.

Staff Sgt. Aaron Kenefick was a personnel specialist with eight years' expertise in administration, so his job was to bring some order to the Afghan personnel procedures and pay records. That sounded like herding cats to me, but he was the man for it, as he cared about doing things right and made you care about it, too.

He would have quite a challenge, as the Afghan Army is not what you would call a tight ship. For example, they have no visible penalty for desertion: soldiers collect their pay, declare themselves on leave, and come back when they run out of money, if they come back at all. Starbucks runs a tighter ship than the Afghan Army. Faced with a turnover of 8 percent per month, molding a fighting unit was almost out of the question. But if anybody could get their records straight, Aaron could.

Doc Layton, our corpsman, would provide some basic medical care to the Afghans in the villages, but his primary job was to be ready in case any advisors or Afghan soldiers were wounded.

I had a job, too: Lt. Johnson put me in charge of tactics, operations, and weapons training. Before each patrol, I approved the Afghan scheme of maneuver, inspected the radios and guns, coordinated fire support, and planned an emergency escape route. This was far easier than planning the sniper missions I had been trained for. I also trained the Askars (Afgahan soldiers) on their M-16 rifles. Some tried to shoot well, and some didn't care. I concentrated on getting across the three basics: take aimed shots and conserve your ammunition—don't fire all over the place in a panic; watch your flanks; listen to your officers. In the middle of a hot shootout, those rules will usually save your life.

On some Marine advisor teams, and all Special Forces teams, everyone is on a first-name basis, regardless of rank. Having the maturity not to overstep your limits is assumed. I didn't call Lt. Johnson by his first name, but we got along well and I rarely called him "sir." He was the boss, and we both knew it.

Aaron, on the other hand, kept a military distance from me. He was a by-the-book staff NCO. Because Lt. Johnson and I had trained together, he may have thought I was a teacher's pet to Lt. Johnson, and it griped him a little.

"We live in the same hooch, Corporal Meyer," he said when I slipped and got too casual, "but don't forget to address me as Staff Sergeant."

"Roger that, Staff Sergeant." I didn't mind that.

"Soon to be Gunnery Sergeant, by the way," he added, smiling. He was excited to make that promotion.

Down at Joyce, Maj. Kevin Williams concentrated on staff matters. He was quiet and pleasant, different from the brusque, hands-on type of commanding officer I knew from the infantry. He let Lt. Johnson manage our team.

Monti, like every U.S. outpost on the frontier, was following the Pentagon's official counterinsurgency strategy. The general idea was to make friends with the villagers, provide them security, give out project money, and build relationships with the local officials. The theory was that when the tribes realized their government was guarding them and giving them things like American-funded generators, they would tell their young men not to join the Taliban. All of us advisors wanted to believe that, but both the American and Afghan soldiers warned us never to assume the villagers were on our side. The Afghans have a saying: you can rent an Afghan but you can never buy one. Meaning they are going to support whoever gives them the most "rent," or money. That was apparent to us within the first week.

There were about forty villages in our area, and the Americans and Afghans at Monti sent out about ten patrols a week, each one planned as carefully as a beer run and executed like one, too. We didn't go out to search and destroy the enemy, although the Afghan soldiers knew which valleys were hostile. We didn't make arrests or bring local police with us because the Askars and the villagers disliked them. The villagers didn't like the Taliban either, but the math didn't add up: ten patrols a week couldn't protect forty villages.

The four of us settled into a routine of patrolling five days a week. The Afghan company commander would pick out a village and we'd rehearse how to make the approach and what to do when we got there. Before leaving we'd check weapons, double-check the operations orders, and test our radio frequencies with the Dog Company op center.

Doc Layton prepared medical supplies to give to the villagers, and Johnson and Staff Sgt. Kenefick rotated as the senior advisor to the Afghans. I manned the turret, alternating between Humvees with .50-caliber machine guns and the Mark 19s with their 40-millimeter guns. The 40-millimeter is a small automatic cannon; its explosive shell, weighing almost one pound, can take apart a cement building.

The Askars climbed into the backs of their Ford Ranger pickups, and we'd leave through the Monti's front gate with about four vehicles. As we drove along, sometimes we'd take potshots from a side valley, and the Askars would pay no attention. Other times, their Rangers skidded to a stop, and we'd pile out and scope the hills for targets we usually couldn't find. On most patrols, we eventually reached a hamlet of ten to forty mud-and-timber houses perched on a hillside, looking one mudslide away from oblivion.

We'd park the trucks and walk up steep, rocky paths where the vehicles couldn't go. The Askars would amble along, not expecting trouble, their weapons dangling casually. We four Americans, of course, were looking everywhere, our fingers beside our triggers and our guns pointing forward—I would have a heavy-duty machine gun at my side. About half of our Afghans were Tajiks from the north who didn't speak the language of the Pashtuns in Kunar. The others were from other tribes, including some from Kunar, though no Afghan soldier in our unit was from the local district. That would put his family at risk, as the Taliban considered Afghan soldiers to be traitors.

Once inside the village, we'd set out sentries and sit down with the elders for a "key leader engagement" over a few cups of hot green tea.

The ritual was predictable:

Lt. Rhula (the Afghan company commander): "Your government wishes to protect you from the dushmen."

The Askars called their enemy dushmen, meaning thugs and bandits. The villagers called them Taliban, but never dushmen. No one called them mujahideen, or holy warriors.

Gray-bearded Elder: "You say this every time you come, but you give us nothing. The last group of Americans promised us a generator. Where is it?"

Lt. Johnson: "We are simple soldiers, like Lt. Rhula. You must speak with the PRT [provincial reconstruction team] about the generator."

Elder: "Americans do nothing but promise."

Lt. Rhula: "Have you seen any strangers?"

Elder: "Taliban sometimes come by. They don't tell us anything. The next village is bad, not us."

It was always the other village. We visited a village for a few hours; the Taliban came and went as they pleased.

Some villages were genuinely friendly, some standoffish. You'd rarely see young men, and any woman would dash inside immediately. The villagers and Askars were polite to one another, but rarely did I see them laugh together or talk in a friendly manner. The Askars looked bored and the villagers looked resigned to casual searches of their compounds while the Afghan officer and the elders sipped tea and we advisors checked off another "key leader engagement."

When we walked into some hamlets, however, you could feel something was wrong. When kids threw rocks at you, you knew what the parents were telling them. Sometimes the Askars grabbed the kids' soccer balls and sliced them apart. This didn't win hearts and minds, but it did stop the rocks. Whenever the elders hurried through the ceremonial tea, though, I'd watch the Askars. When any soldier senses danger, he crouches down a few inches to make himself less of a target. When the Askars did that, I went on full alert.

Hafez was our lead interpreter and, we quickly learned, our best warning system. A thirty-seven-year-old sergeant major retired from the Afghan Army, Hafez had served in Kunar for three years with advisor teams. The Afghan soldiers distrusted him because he refused to support their never-ending schemes to skim from the Americans.

Hafez was a man without a country. His request for a visa to the States went unanswered because he lacked a high-level American sponsor. Yet his loyalty to Americans was unbounded. He taught us how to act with the elders, provided tips before meetings, and pointed out when the Askars were taking advantage of us or when the villagers were lying. Hafez became the unofficial fifth member of our team. Inside a hamlet, if he shook his head at us, we knew it was time to forget the tea and get out.

Lt. Rhula was smart. To him and to the Askars, the war was a job. If they were rounded up or killed, their families would lose a steady paycheck. Most wouldn't stay to fight on ground that favored the enemy.

The dushmen weren't idiots either. Think of it. You're three or four Taliban living in a compound, and you see pickups bouncing over the rocks toward your village. It's another "key leader engagement" by the infidels and the Afghan traitor soldiers.

Unseen, you run up the hill and dig up your two AK rifles and a PKM machine gun with fifty rounds in the belt. From behind some rocks, you squint down at the helmet of an American advisor in an armored turret, slowly cranking his enormous .50-caliber gun back and forth, not knowing where you are, but knowing you are watching him.

Usually the dushmen waited until we drove away before firing in sheer bravado. Thank you and don't come again. I'd respond by turning the offending hillside into dust clouds. Only two or three times did I hit somebody. Usually it was just a cloud of dust downrange and the wind-chimey cascade of empty brass shells falling into the Humvee from my thumping gun. Then we'd head back to Monti.

The Askars with us didn't care one way or another about our counterinsurgency theory. They were soldiers, with no attachment to the people living around Monti. For them, it was another day, another walk through a hamlet, then back to base for dinner, chats over their cell phones, some fine hash to smoke, then a few hours' sleep in the barracks. They joked with one another and posted security, bored bit players in a drama that changed only when a friend went home or took a bullet. I learned to trust and rely on them every day. They became like family.

Over the course of these patrols, I went through thousands of rounds, but it's hard to hit an unseen enemy. Not that I didn't try. Lt. Johnson gave me a long leash to determine team tactics, and sometimes I let my hunting instincts get the better of me. I kept hearing about this place called Dab Valley, where every patrol took fire. So I came up with a brilliant plan and presented it in low-key fashion to Lt. Johnson. We'd drive up toward Dab, I explained, and then stop any passing vehicles to search for weapons or ammo. I didn't tell him that we were going to park at the exact spot where previous patrols came under fire. I was quite proud of my scheme. When we came under fire, I'd train my Askars, just as headquarters wanted, and shoot Taliban, just as I wanted.

So we drove into this narrow gulch and stopped. When we looked up, we could see a dozen caves where the enemy could be hiding. We sat for a few minutes knowing we were sitting ducks. I happily waited to unload with my .50-caliber. Lt. Johnson, though, was taking in the bigger picture, including what would happen if an RPG blew off one of our tires and we were stuck in the shooting gallery. The more he looked around, the more he growled at me. Finally, he threw up his hands and shouted that we were leaving. In a cloud of dust, we drove out of that death trap.

"Meyer," he said, "why do I let you talk me into insane things?"

Chapter 4

ADVISING

A few days later—early August—I had another chance to impress Lt. Johnson with my initiative. We were on our way to conduct a key leader engagement. When we stopped at this small hamlet, we were greeted with a mortar shell exploding next to us. I scanned the ridgeline and saw the dust raised by the recoil of the launching tube, about a thousand meters away.

We took cover. There were maybe two or three guys up there. We started calling in artillery and we could have driven away, of course, but what fun would that be?

Instead, I came up with another brilliant idea.

"Let me climb up and flank them from the left," I said to Johnson. He stared up at the mountain, thinking about it. To show him how confident I was, I grabbed a few Askars and started climbing before he could say no.

It took twenty minutes for us to scramble up, with only a couple of hostile rounds cracking off the rocks near us. When we reached the top, we looked around for the mortar team.

Suddenly, heavy slugs cracked overhead. It was friendly fire, coming from the Afghan police station position in the town on the other side of the mountain. They had spotted our silhouettes and figured we were the mortar guys. They were dialing us into the crosshairs of a Russian anti-aircraft gun, which would soon turn the ridge, and us, to dust.

"Get it off us!" I radioed frantically.

Lt. Johnson pulled out his cell phone and called Lt. Rhula, who immediately called the Afghan police chief.

"If your guys fire one more burst," Rhula yelled, "I'll drop mortars on your head."

The firing stopped. We stood up, dusted off, and trudged back down the hill.

"If you'd gotten clipped, Meyer," Lt. Johnson said, "I'd have to spend a month with investigators."

"I had it under control, sir."

"Uh-huh."

A few days later, Rhula filled two Ranger trucks with Askars and sped out the gate without telling us where he was going. He said he was responding to an ambush of several jingle trucks. Most Afghan trucks are brightly painted and decorated with jingling bells, as if every vehicle had to pass through a third-grade art class. But if all your life you've been saving for that vehicle, you want to show it off. Trucks were routinely stopped by Taliban or other bandits and shaken down. Sometimes the Taliban torched the trucks for no obvious reason. The truck drivers continuously played Russian roulette.

About an hour after Rhula left the gate, we got a call from a helicopter pilot.

"Hey, Fox 6, your Afghans are shooting it out with some Afghan security guards," the pilot said. "What do you want me to do?"

"We have no SA," Lt. Johnson replied. "Don't do anything."

"No SA" means no situational awareness—a military phrase meaning no fucking idea what is happening. An hour later, our Askars returned with bullet holes in their trucks. Eventually we found out they had driven off the ambushers and, as payment for their services, had siphoned five gallons of gas from a jingle truck. The pissed-off drivers had shot at Rhula's Humvees as they drove away. No one was seriously hurt, though—only a couple scratches and bruises. All good.

"We won't help you steal," Lt. Johnson said.

"I don't know what you're talking about!" Rhula said.

Hafez shook his head, and so did the others. We had busted them and they saw the humor in it. If one of them had been killed, though, it would have been different.

The four of us adopted a stray mutt named Annie. She was always happy to see us barge in, peel off our armor, and open the ammo box we kept full of dog biscuits. For some of the U.S. Army guys, our small hooch was a hangout because the atmosphere was relaxed. Lt. Johnson treated everyone as an equal and kept things upbeat. I don't mean to say it was summer camp, but it was good to get to know each other, despite the differences of rank and age and upbringing.

Lt. Johnson was a Virginian by birth but was now Mr. Oregon. That's where he saw his future. He was in tremendous shape and at sunset, would muster us out for a hundred push-ups, two hundred sit-ups, and ten laps around the perimeter.

Soon-to-be Gunnery Sgt. Kenefick, a New Yorker, looked like a damn movie star—maybe Ben Affleck. He worked day and night to get the Askars shaped up organizationally. He had been a high school quarterback and had wanted to be a Marine way before 9/11.

Hospitalman 3rd Class James "Doc" Layton, the Californian, with a younger, happier face than the rest of us, and heavy-metal music in his earbuds, was watching out for our health (according to him) and bringing health services to the villages we visited. Doc had grown up in a small town near Modesto, and as a teen he would walk the several miles into town each night to work in a pizza joint. He had planned out his life on those long walks. He was going to pursue a career in radiology while operating a little recording studio on the side.

As for me, I didn't think about civilian life after the war, and I wasn't ready to settle down. I was training the Askars to use the M16 rifle and riding shotgun on our daily patrols to hold "key leader engagements." Lt. Rhula appeared to want to do the right things, and his first sergeant was tough and demanding. But they couldn't impose their wills on the entire company. The Askars had a high sense of individual self-worth and tolerated each other like an unruly class of tough eighth-graders. When an Afghan soldier went home without permission—what I would call deserting the unit—the others weren't upset. We were advising an army with no established standards of group behavior.

Sometimes we advisors felt more like parole officers. Some Askars tried, and others clung to old habits, like—what can we steal today? A standard scam was to siphon fuel from their own generator and their own trucks to sell in the local markets. So we parked the Afghan Humvees on the U.S. side of the motor pool and let their generators run out of fuel. After two days of no lights, no air conditioning, no hot water, and no rides to the market, they got the message and behaved themselves—for a while.

They grew hash wherever they could. When a stoned Askar stumbled or staggered on patrol, the others would smile tolerantly. "Hash cigarettes are like dushman RPGs," Johnson warned. "If you're high, you can't shoot back and the RPGs will kill you." When Lt. Johnson burned the plants growing on base, the Askars retaliated by making a hash run into the market and, stoned silly, crashed two Humvees on their way back.

What bugged me most was the negligent discharge of guns. They would play with their new guns at night until one went off. I'd hear the crack of it, then nervous laughter. I'd storm through the camp until I smelled the cordite hanging in the air. Then I'd grab the offender and bang on the door of Lt. Rhula's hooch. He would take it from there.

In the hills along the Pakistani border, no Afghan, military or civilian, had much of anything. I think practically every American soldier or Marine tried to help in some way. We purchased candy and trinkets in the markets to give to the kids. I soon had two little buddies, boys about ten or eleven. They'd hang around the main gate, yelling "Meyeda! Meyeda!" (Meyer!) when they saw me. At first, I'd buy them Cokes, and then I started sharing my care packages from home—soap, candy, peanuts, gum. Maybe a decade from now, some kids would remember that some Americans were kind to them, even when their older brothers were shooting at them. Maybe not. You don't help out because you expect something in return.

If people like you, generally you like them. I enjoyed hanging out with the Askars. They laughed a lot at little, and once you were firm about not being Santa Claus, most stopped asking you for stuff. I ate dinner every night with them—rice, kachaloo potatoes, and gravy. Of about a hundred Askars, I memorized the names of the twenty or so who tried the hardest. I was especially close with five who were as dedicated to their job as I was. We'd sit outside in the evenings with our food and, with Hafez's help, talk for hours. They refused to believe that my dad worked three hundred acres in his spare time, after he got home from work. How many days a week, they asked, did I rent a tractor? They were convinced I was a millionaire when I told them we had two tractors.

They thought it was a great joke when I told them my government paid farmers not to raise tobacco. Making money by not working was beyond their comprehension. When we sketched out in the dirt the comparative size of our farms, they decided that, yes, I was the richest man they had ever met. They were absolutely dumbfounded why a man so wealthy would come to Afghanistan to fight bandits.

I asked if it was true that they shared their houses with their cows. Certainly not, they said; cows were kept in a separate section of the house, not in the living quarters.

Sex with women intrigued them. I won't get into what they asked about, but their sexual imaginations knew no bounds. Whatsoever.

I discussed religion with them all the time, trying to understand their beliefs while they were doing the same about mine. I was surprised at how educated they were about Christianity.

The Askars scoffed at the suggestion that the Taliban were the true Muslims. They were just bandits and murderers, they said. I don't think they said that just for my benefit. When I asked if they knew where the dushmen were living, they assured me they did. But when I urged that we attack them there, they laughed as if I were simpleminded. I was always talking to them about how badly I wanted to fight and how much I looked forward to it. They would just sit and laugh, nodding along, with about as much confidence in me as they had in the idea that there would ever be peace in Afghanistan.

. . .

After dinner was a good time to call home, as people would be just starting their day in the States. We bought minutes on inexpensive Afghan cell phones. I wasn't much for emails or video chats—I just never felt comfortable or natural communicating that way. A phone call was about my limit.

"Hi, Dad, this is Dakota. How'd your week go?"

"Good. The rain's held off and we got up a hundred bales behind Pepa's house. Tractor's acting up. What're you doing?"

"Nothing much. Just got back from another patrol. Pretty boring."

It was like that. I would also call my friends Toby and Ann. Ann had been my high school advisor and she and her husband and I were like family. Toby wouldn't hang up until he got something out of me that was either funny or dangerous. They would talk about me and what they saw in the news about that strange country in far-off central Asia.

In our hooch, we didn't talk much about our lives back home. It was another planet, and nobody was interested in the soap operas going on back in somebody else's family. We weren't bored or annoyed by each other. We were different ranks and ages, so the verbal hazing you'd hear among lance corporals in a platoon—ridiculing comments about families, wives, or girlfriends—didn't happen. When we visited another base, we stayed together.

After a while, it all becomes you, your buddies, and your Afghan friends. Other worlds fade away, even the other advisors ten miles down the road at Joyce. You stay alive because of what you do each day, sometimes each hour. It's just you and your small band, operating beyond the bounds of civilization. You even think you control your own destiny.

Chapter 5

COMING TOGETHER

Some U.S. soldiers at Monti confided to us that they weren't seeing enough action. After several outposts had been overrun, the U.S. high command had tightened the rules about leaving the wire. A patrol had to write a briefing detailed enough for a space launch. However, since we advisors fell under the Afghan command we could still plan our normal patrols—the beer runs with badass vehicles.

Sgt. 1st Class Dennis Jeffords complained to me that he wasn't getting enough action. One night he and PFC Lage pulled me aside. Lage liked to fight so much that he carried a 240G machine gun instead of a rifle. Jeffords had received permission to set up a vehicle control point the next day. Nothing was more boring than a VCP—stopping jingle trucks and searching through chickens and fertilizer poop for weapons that were never found.

Jeffords and Lage had decided to place their checkpoint at Hill 1911, a notorious ambush point where a steep valley intersected with the only paved road north from Monti. Their plan was to sit there until they took fire. Then, instead of pulling back as standing orders required, they would stand and fight against the enemy on the high ground.

"We may need backup," he said. "But if I ask over there"—he pointed toward his op center—"I'll be ordered not to go. So be ready to roll early if you want in on the action."

Sgt. Jeffords was known for being the crazy one on base when it came to fighting the enemy. Guys always talked about the time he walked up Dab Valley with a big bright orange air panel—made to mark your position for aircraft—on his back as a cape trying to get the Taliban to shoot at him. I wanted to do the exact same thing except *while* getting shot at. I briefed Lt. Johnson on my latest scheme.

"Meyer," he said. "That is a bullshit idea. You'll get me in trouble again. Forget about it."

At six in the morning, Jeffords came up on the radio, and I could hear shooting in the background.

"We're engaged," he said. "You coming?"

I shook Lt. Johnson awake. He muttered that Jeffords' platoon would break contact, as was standard procedure. He rolled over to go back to sleep. I shook him again.

"I don't think so," I said. "We gotta get out there, sir—something must be wrong, and you know how long it takes the Army to react."

I added a little drama to get his wheels spinning. Mumbling, he got dressed. I was like a dog with his owner's leash in his mouth, demanding his morning walk. I even held open the Humvee door for my groggy lieutenant. Together with two truckloads of excited Askars, we rolled to Hill 1911, where Jeffords had deployed his dismounted platoon. As usual, the dushmen were high up on the ridge, shooting and scooting among huge boulders.

"I can climb up," I said, "and flank them from the right."

Jeffords nodded vigorously in agreement, smiling. Lt. Johnson gave me a skeptical look.

"All right, Meyer, do your grunt thing."

I grabbed six or seven Askars and started climbing. Halfway up, a grenade burst next to me, but the rocky ground deflected its shrapnel. I didn't think the dushmen were that close. We hit the deck, not able to see them. Over the radio, Lt. Johnson informed me that it wasn't a dushmen grenade; it was friendly fire. A soldier had fired a 40-millimeter shell, not able to tell us from the dushmen. So this was my chance. I pulled a high-visibility orange air panel from my pack, draped it over my shoulders, and continued climbing.

By the time we reached the top, the dushmen had pulled back to our left. We dared not run single file along the ridge trail, so we stayed where we were. Jeffords' platoon continued plastering the hillside to our front. The dushmen replied with plunging fire, scattering rock chips in all directions and nicking several soldiers. Fortunately, no one needed a medevac. Within an hour, the dushmen had evaporated, per usual.

My little flanking party, thoroughly exhausted, walked back downhill. Jeffords was pleased with his caper, and his soldiers were all grins. They had fired a few thousand rounds, aired out their cabin fever, and nobody was hit too badly. Lt. Johnson was less than pleased. The whole thing went against standard procedures. And he knew I had been a party to it.

"Meyer," he said, "I told you this was bullshit. I don't know how you finagled me into this again."

Just before the Afghan presidential election in late August of 2009, Lt. Johnson sent Staff Sgt. Kenefick and me, along with some Askars, to guard the polling station at Dangam, a district center on the Pakistan border. President Karzai's cronies had already rigged the election. Dangam was one of many remote districts guaranteed to deliver more votes than there were voters. What a country!

Staff Sgt. Kenefick and I were still a little standoffish with each other about his by-the-book ways. Maybe the lieutenant was forcing us to work together, or he was exiling me so he could relax for a few days. Dangam had been the patrol area for Lt. Jake Kerr's platoon. Kerr was the wild-bunch officer at Monti, a loaded pistol who did what he wanted. I heard that at West Point he had played rugby, which is football without a helmet. He had sometimes come to our hooch to borrow, like a cup of sugar, a powerful weapon for one operation or another. Jacked from too many years in the weight room, Kerr tromped around the hills like an angry bear, and his platoon adopted his edgy style.

Early on, his platoon was sent to Dangam to stop the infiltration from Pakistan. Kerr's soldiers had hiked up to every *khol,* or small knot of houses, along the road from Monti out to Dangam, to offer jobs to pave the road and build schools. Kerr spread the pay equally among small competing tribes. In turn, the work crews, not wanting to be blown up, pointed out where the IEDs were hidden. In short, Kerr knew how to play the tribal game.

In retaliation, the Taliban sent a raiding party to attack the Dangam district office. Tipped off, Kerr had a machine-gun crew waiting on a nearby hill. Three attackers were killed, and the others retreated back into Pakistan. In appreciation, the local Mushani tribe invited the Americans to a feast, where they welcomed Kerr as a tribal member and gave him the name Zelaware Zelmae, or Brave Son.

Kerr persuaded the local Askars and police to help his platoon build a fort. Once that was hardened, he planned to set up ambushes along the trails leading to Pakistan, a mile farther east. But when a nearby outpost was overrun in May, Army headquarters pulled Kerr's platoon out of Dangam because it was "too exposed." The platoon thought headquarters had overreacted.

Staff Sgt. Kenefick and I took fifteen Askars and drove out to Dangam. We settled into Kerr's old fort on top of a small hill with sheer sides protected by triple rows of barbed wire. The fort was a small patch of flat ground surrounded by a deep trench line, with bunkers at each corner—impossible to assault on foot.

But several hundred meters away on all sides were towering mountains. The dushmen could climb higher than the fort and fire down RPGs. It's hard to find the highest peak in a country jammed full of mountains. You'd have to go all the way east to Everest if you didn't want any higher ground around you.

Kerr had compensated by pre-plotting every visible slope, so he could call in artillery fire like calling for a takeout pizza. So I did the same. Before leaving Monti, I plotted a half dozen Kilo Echoes. KEs are pre-calibrated impact points for artillery fire. If we came under attack, I could radio a command like, "Left one hundred meters from KE 3366, fire for effect." The artillery rounds zoomed the five miles over the mountain to that exact spot. Targeting in mountainous elevations is tricky, but I had sufficient practice during sniper training to feel comfortable.

When we arrived about noon, after a long drive without saying much to each other, Staff Sgt. Kenefick and I assigned two Askars to each bunker. I then took out my binoculars, map, and compass to recheck the Kilo Echoes. I had been doing this for about half an hour when a sheep or goat herder in a bluish man-dress walked into plain sight, about four hundred meters away on a higher hillside. He was waving a walking stick at his invisible sheep, while looking right at me. His cover was so pathetic that I almost waved back at him. Then he ducked behind an outcropping, stuck the barrel of an AK out of the rocks, and fired off four or five rounds.

Staff Sgt. Kenefick was standing outside a bunker about a hundred feet from me.

"Meyer, we're under attack!" he yelled.

Technically, yes. But the shepherd was shooting without poking his head up to aim. He had one chance in a thousand of hitting us. A second harmless burst followed, the bullets cracking more than ten feet above our heads.

"Call for arty! NOW!" Staff Sgt. Kenefick yelled, holding the radio headset out toward me.

Oh, nice. Staff Sgt. soon-to-be Gunnery Sgt. Kenefick needed the lowly corporal's help. I trotted toward him, stopped, assumed parade-rest posture, arms locked behind my back, chest pushed forward in the wide open, and pasted a respectful expression on my face.

"What does the staff sergeant wish the corporal to do?"

Another burst from the AK.

"This is no time to be a smart-ass, Meyer!"

A few more rounds, still way high. I'm locked in parade rest.

"Aye, Staff Sergeant."

He balanced the handset, considering whether to throw it at me.

"Meyer, hurry up!"

He had started calling in the artillery mission, and when I got to him he was asking me, "What do I say now?"

"Left one hundred, drop two hundred," I said.

He repeated it on the radio.

"What now?" he asked.

"Fire for effect," I said, "should be dead on."

"Okay, fire for effect," he repeated over the radio.

We settled behind some sandbags. Even before the shells landed, two of our Askars rushed up with their brand-new 203s, which are short, wide-barreled weapons that fire 40-millimeter grenades the size of a man's fist. They plunked a few shells toward the shepherd and puffs of orange powder bloomed across the hillside. By mistake, the Askars were shooting training rounds, not explosive rounds.

The shepherd scampered away. If he is still alive, he probably enlivens campfires in the Hindu Kush with his account of gas warfare. In old age, he will blame his ailments on a chemical weapon that was a mixture of talcum powder and red dye.

The artillery rounds landed right on target. After the fire had ended, Staff Sgt. Kenefick looked at me and slapped me on the back.

"I'm pretty good at that, aren't I!" he said.

We both burst out laughing. Somehow that stupid incident broke the tension between us. Over the next few days, we learned how to divide the tasks and work together.

Dangam, a dusty border hamlet, had changed allegiances several times in the long war. The border meant nothing to the tribes. Smugglers, commuters, Taliban, local cops—everyone seemed to get along, like in the intergalactic bar in *Star Wars*. We couldn't figure out much of what was going on. Dodd Ali, my closest Askar friend, said he and the other Askars were outsiders like us, so they had no idea who might be Taliban.

I watched the town's daily routines. The sub-governor calmly went to work inside the district compound below our outpost. The police chief puttered around in his truck, as though he didn't have a care in the world. Night after night we saw the bobbing flashlights going over the pass into Pakistan. We didn't have a clue who was coming or going, or why.

Our Askars insisted the Taliban were skirting around our outpost. They pointed at figures about seven hundred meters away, walking single-file, and shouted, "Dushmen! Dushmen!" Our rules of engagement required that any target display both hostile capability, like a rifle, and hostile intent, like aiming at us. I couldn't plug someone for walking single-file. While we watched the district compound from one hilltop, insurgents were watching from other hilltops and chatting on their handheld radios. Our Askars said they used simple codes, like "the chickens [mortars] and horses [rockets] are in position."

At Lt. Johnson's insistence, Dog Company had sent out a squad from Monti to stand guard with us on election day. Jeffords' squad brought a badminton set from a care package from the States. We decided to set it up on the helo landing zone, the most exposed place on base, and have a tournament. We called it the No Taliban Badminton Tournament 2009, and we swatted the shuttlecock back and forth, hoping to lure a dushmen into shooting.

Dodd Ali asked if he could shoot the shuttlecock out of the air with his squad automatic weapon, which shoots ten rounds a second. I said no; if he missed with the SAW, I'd be splattered all over the sandbags. I was "Meyetta" to Dodd Ali. He couldn't believe I had ridden on the back of my cow, Tinker Bell. He was fun to talk to, open, friendly, and fearless. We would sit around talking and asking questions of each other like kids in middle school, learning as much as we could about each other. He proudly cleaned his SAW five times a day and absorbed every tip I gave him about shooting. He was the most disciplined Askar on base. That's why we gave him the SAW in the first place.

Staff Sgt. Kenefick and I figured the local officials were crazy to have announced the voting location in advance. The night before the elections, we therefore switched the voting station to a small store outside of town. We sent the Askars into town at morning prayer to redirect the voters.

The insurgents liked to shoot 107-millimeter rockets—light, three-foot-long projectiles fired from short tubes that were set up rapidly on temporary bipods. A man can carry a launcher on his back, and the rocket can be aimed directly at the target. The damn things can go five miles.

The voting started at 7 A.M. I heard the first rocket *foomp* at 7:01. It ripped apart the front of the empty district compound where a hundred voters would have been lined up had we not moved them a kilometer away. The empty center took twenty-one rounds in the next two hours. The Taliban had their orders to hit that building, so they did, stupidly, again and again. But they hit it well.

I left Dangam with a healthy respect for the skill of the rocket gunners and their cold hearts, willing to kill their own relatives. They didn't do so this day, but they'd tried.

Staff Sgt. Kenefick and I headed back to Monti, while the over-full ballot box headed for Kabul. Staff Sgt. Kenefick and I were okay with each other. Absolutely.

Chapter 6

OUT OF THE SMOKE

A few weeks later, it was Combat Outpost Monti's turn to feel the full force of the rockets. In early September, just before dinner one evening I heard the *foomp, foomp* of two rockets launched from tubes somewhere up on the hill above us. We started taking concentrated rocket fire on the Afghan side of the base. We had taken RPG shots before, of course, but several rockets incoming barrage-style was a new experience. The dushmen were firing on a direct lay from a hilltop to the southeast, with the gunners looking straight down at Monti.

They were in the air, screeching our way with their very rocket-like sound. You don't have time to react. The hair on the back of your neck tingles for a split second before the bang. I jumped on the .50-cal and pumped out rounds, while Lt. Johnson tried to lay an azimuth for our mortars. Then my gun jammed.

The lieutenant and I ran into the concrete watchtower at the main gate to get another gun. No sooner had I hopped on a 240 machine gun than a rocket shook the tower. An Askar picked up an RPG to shoot out the other window. I grabbed it out of his hands and placed it under my feet. The back-blast in that enclosed space would have fried us. I shouted down at Doc Layton to start shooting back. You need to get your firepower going if you want to keep the enemy from popping up and firing. It's all about volume, aggression, overpowering them with a flood of bullets and explosions.

"I'm a doc!" he yelled back. In our previous skirmishes, he had been there to patch us up, not to kill anybody.

"C'mon, Doc. Corpsmen can shoot back when they need to!" I yelled.

He started firing his peashooter M4 rifle toward the dushmen moving on the hill at least seven hundred meters away, probably setting up more rockets. A ridiculous range for the M4. We heard a sudden screech before another rocket slammed into the side of the tower. An Askar tapped me on the shoulder. He had a shocked look on his face and was pointing down. The bone was sticking out of his right shin where his foot had been, and blood was gushing out.

"Doc Layton, put a tourniquet on this!" I screamed. Doc had something better to do now, the thing he had come for.

I gestured at two Askars to carry the wounded man down the metal outside stairs. Twice they dropped him as more rockets slammed in. Lt. Johnson saw that they were just killing the guy and he jumped up to take care of the situation. Doc Layton grabbed the 240 and started ripping off bursts as I put the wounded man over my shoulder and headed down the stairs. Halfway down, a rocket hit a truck next to the tower. I leapt the last flight of stairs and landed hard on the ground. Lt. Johnson ran out and stopped a Ford Ranger that was headed out of the area.

Lt. Johnson was screaming at our Askars to return fire. The rockets had them spooked. I lowered the wounded man into the truck bed. Lt. Johnson calmed down the driver and the Ranger drove toward the med station.

I climbed back up the tower to help Doc Layton, who was still blasting away with the 240. I turned around on the steps to see Johnson sprinting across the base to the mortar pit. A shriek and boom followed—a rocket hit the tree next to Johnson. I was okay, but I was sure it must have got the lieutenant. You can't process what you just saw, or think you saw. But a few seconds later he emerged black-faced from the smoke, brushing off his clothes. We laughed about it as we kept shooting. I took over the 240 from Doc Layton. An enemy PKM machine gun had joined the fight, and some rounds were pinging off the tower. The enemy's Russian PKMs and our 240s are a match, both shooting .308-caliber bullets at a rate of about 750 per minute.

"Where's Staff Sgt. Kenefick?" I yelled.

Doc Layton pointed toward the northeast tower.

"Get over there and stay with him!" I yelled.

Suicide bombers sometimes rushed the wire, trying to take an infidel with them as they evaporated in a red flash. Without hesitating, Doc Layton ran down the stairs, across the open space, and into the tower with Staff Sgt. Kenefick. Two or three seconds later, a rocket slammed into their bunker, exploding to pieces an Afghan worker huddled there beside the sandbags. Smoke rolled out of the tower.

"They're gone!" I yelled to Johnson, not believing what I had just seen.

I resumed firing. It's all you can do. The best first aid at that point was to return fire. Johnson worked the radio.

"Fox 3–1, Fox 3–1, this is Fox 3, Staff Sgt. Kenefick, Doc Layton . . . Come on, man! Answer up!"

We kept firing, but it seemed unworldly now. We were on automatic. Lt. Johnson got on the radio again.

"Three-1, Fox 3–1, this is Fox 3, Staff Sgt. Kenefick, Doc Layton . . . Come on, man! Answer up!"

Then finally . . .

"Yeah, yeah, this is 3–1. We're good."

Ten minutes later, our attack helicopters began their strafing runs—low, rumbling *brrr*s, like a giant burping. Incredible firepower, those lovely birds. Enemy fire ceased. Attack over.

Johnson and I ran over to the smoking bunker, as Staff Sgt. Kenefick and Doc Layton stumbled out. The four of us sat on the bloody sandbags in the growing dusk, talking about it. Their eyes were slightly glazed and wide, wide open.

As a grunt, I was resigned about death. I don't go to church. To me, organized religions seem like bureaucracies. But I believed in God. Grunts see His acts on the battlefield. Guys beside you get shot or blown up. You don't. God has a plan that we won't understand until we cross to the other side. There's no sense obsessing about getting tagged. Either a bullet has your name on it or it doesn't. No need for philosophizing.

Lt. Johnson, Staff Sgt. Kenefick, and Doc Layton, though, weren't infantry. They had considered that by coming to Afghanistan they might die, but it hadn't kicked in until now. Now they had heard the screams and seen the blood. Everybody, soot-covered, understood that now—that if we went home together, it might not be alive.

The Askars were cleaning up the bloody mess not six feet from us, taking away the ripped-up body of their friend.

We mumbled some stuff. All of us were too embarrassed to talk about our feelings, but we knew what we were all thinking: this shit was for real, and there were only the four of us.

"We'll be there for each other," Doc Layton said.

The surfer dude surprised me. He had said the one thing that made any sense.

Chapter 7

GANJIGAL

We were always solid, but now it was as if we were stitched together, even while each of us thought the other three were hilarious nut cases. Lt. Johnson prowled the Afghan barracks, determined to stamp out the "RPG cigarettes." Doc Layton, who'd never had a short haircut in his life, had decided that while his real calling was saving lives, you can't do that if you're dead. From now on, he was shooting back without waiting to be told. Staff Sgt. Kenefick was insufferable. His beloved Yankees had gone on a two-month tear and seemed destined for the World Series. Every time they won, he acted like he had been in the game. The staff sergeant also fancied himself quite the basketball player. I couldn't wait to get him on a court and dunk the ball over his head. Then I'd hustle off before he discovered that was my one and only basketball move.

It wasn't long after the rocket attack that we received a call saying we were needed at FOB Joyce to run a mission in the morning. We started prepping to go when we were told to stand by; the mission had been pushed back another day. Lt. Johnson told me to prepare to move our Afghan company down to Joyce. He wasn't told what the mission was due to operational security.

I checked the ammo and water loads for our sixty-odd Askars. Whatever was ahead, it wasn't a big deal. I figured it would be one more useless "key leader engagement" in one more mountain village, like dozens of others.

In the afternoon of September 7, 2009, our convoy of about eight vehicles drove south. When we got to Joyce we found out that our mission was to provide security for a key leader engagement in a mountain village named Ganjigal. Ganjigal lay two miles north of Joyce and we drove right by the mouth of the valley. Ganjigal sounded like the name of an Irish town, full of smiling faces and friendly pubs. I could see a few of the larger compounds far back on a hillside, nestled against steep ridgelines.

"Bad place," Hafez muttered. "Bad people."

That got my attention. Hafez, who knew every village in Kunar, rarely pointed one out as more hostile than the others. It didn't make me fearful, but my antennae were raised. I was suddenly more aware of my gunnery mission as it related to the team.

Located two miles north of Joyce, Ganjigal Valley was an infiltration corridor from next-door Pakistan. Video from night cameras on unmanned aerial vehicles showed donkey trains wending their way up to the border, smuggling out cedar planks and bringing in arms. You couldn't call a fire mission on donkeys and shepherds, though, and U.S. patrols rarely ventured up the valley, because Battalion 1–32 was overextended protecting the main convoy routes.

Occasional shots from the valley were fired at passing U.S. convoys. Yet unarmed Askars casually walked to a market just outside the valley, with no fear of being targeted. The local understanding seemed to be: don't bother us, and we won't bother you.

. . .

A few weeks earlier the local truce had broken down. Rockets fired from the ridge above Ganjigal had ignited a huge fuel fire inside Joyce. Fearing retaliation, Ganjigal elders trooped down to Joyce for a *shura,* or a palaver. They proposed that the Americans hire workers from Ganjigal and pay for a tribal militia that would stop the rockets. The Afghan border police commander, Lt. Col. Ayoub, believed the villagers were mostly Taliban, and he reacted angrily to what he understood as a demand bribe to stop the rockets.

"These Americans aren't Russians," he told them. "They didn't bomb you after you burned their base. They owe you nothing for your bad behavior."

Battalion 1–32, not amused at being shaken down, threatened to build an outpost in the valley, thus stopping all smuggling across the border, which would have devastated the local economy. After thinking that over, the elders returned a few days later and issued verbal support for the government over the provincial public radio. Capt. Ray Kaplan, the 1–32 assistant intelligence officer, was skeptical of their motives.

"The Taliban approved the radio broadcast," Kaplan said, "maybe to get goodies in return for an empty gesture. Those who spoke on the radio could be goat herders for all we know, with zero status inside the village."

In early September, a U.S. patrol entered a hamlet near Ganjigal to test the reaction of the locals. The villagers seemed friendly. When the patrol left, only a few PKM machine-gun rounds were fired at them. So the effort was deemed a success. Inside 1–32, the view was that Ganjigal was "pro-U.S. and supportive of the Afghan government."

The elders then asked that Afghan—not American—soldiers visit Ganjigal and provide money for their mosque. So our key leader engagement was scheduled for September 7—and was then pushed back a day. Most Afghan males—whether merchants, villagers, police, or soldiers—had cell phones, and they jabbered constantly. The delay was equivalent to announcing our movement over the public radio.

The four of us on Team Monti, together with about ten other advisors in the command orbit of Joyce, attended the mission brief. Few Afghans or soldiers from 1–32 were present; they had been briefed separately. Second Lt. Fabayo briefed Operation Buri Booza, or Dancing Goat II. He used only one slide, showing a photomap of the valley. Coming on top of Hafez's warning, the map clearly showed a trap. (See map.) We were walking into a box canyon surrounded by high ridgelines. The horseshoe-shaped valley provided the ideal shooting gallery for snipers and machine-gun crews. I would have planned to go in there with heavy guns, armor, and air cover.

The village of Ganjigal consisted of two small hamlets separated by a gravel wash. The plan was to advance from the west up the wash and turn left into North Ganjigal, about fifty compounds stacked one on top of another on a steep hillside right beneath a massive ridgeline that ran back into Pakistan. The largest compound consisted of a concrete foundation with half-completed walls.

On the other side of the wash, on a steep finger of land, South Ganjigal held about fifteen compounds enclosed behind stout mud walls. Farther south was another wash, then another wall of rock ridgeline. A school funded by the United States was perched on its slope. Constructed of thick stones anchored in heavy cement, the

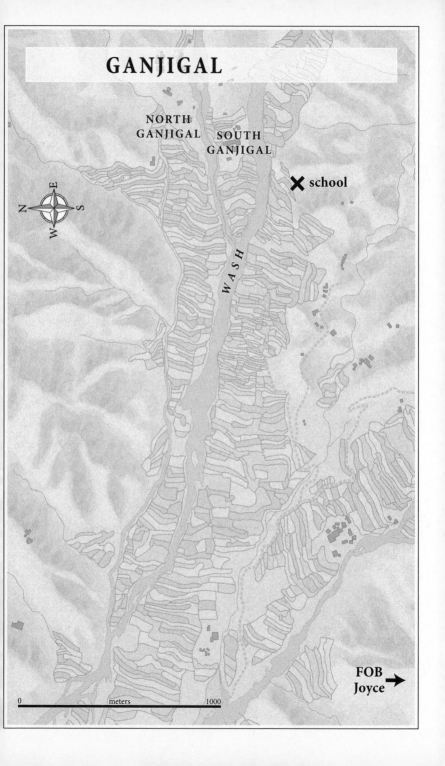

GANJIGAL

NORTH
GANJIGAL

SOUTH
GANJIGAL

✕ school

N
E
W
S

WASH

FOB
Joyce

0 meters 1000

school could withstand avalanches, blizzards, floods, or machine-gun fire. Despite American offers to pay for teachers, the school had been empty for three years. The villagers claimed their children had to work, leaving no time for school.

Two miles south of all that was Camp Joyce, with its 120-millimeter mortars at ready; 120s were fearsome shells that dropped straight down and smashed anything in their path.

"There are reports of ten to twenty Taliban, maybe more," Fabayo said. "The likely course of action is that they shoot at us as we pull out. That's what happened to 1–32 on their patrol up there a few days ago."

Historically the Taliban had not sprung ambushes from inside villages, so that wasn't discussed at the briefing. Plus, we were going in with ninety Afghans and fifteen advisors, with a platoon from 1–32 deployed behind us as a quick reaction force.

"This show belongs to our Afghan counterparts," Fabayo said. "We advisors will stand off to the side and let them talk with the elders. We're not in the lead. We're assisting."

That made no sense, I thought. Considering who was doing the briefing and who was hearing it, we were in the tactical lead, even if we claimed otherwise. No Afghan had a clue how to call in the 120 mortars. I had been over this ground before with Maj. Williams and Fabayo. I'm not good at hiding my feelings, and I may have shaken my head in disagreement during the brief.

It was nuts to rely upon indirect 120 mortar fire alone. One look at the valley dictated bringing the direct firepower mounted on our armored Humvees. Don't bring a knife to a gunfight; bring a cannon. The land sloped up so steeply that houses were supported by those below them. The compounds were made of stone, concrete, and adobe bricks baked by centuries of summers. They looked like a set of interlocking gun pillboxes.

Outside each main house was a small dirt courtyard with an out-house, a clothesline, a clay cooking oven, and a few stalls for the cows and donkeys. Scrawny barnyard fowl and mean watchdogs ran loose. High mud walls enclosed every compound, separated by twisting footpaths littered with human and animal feces. Inside this rat's nest of alleyways, a man could walk from one end of the village to the other without being seen and fully protected against small-arms fire. Big, boomerang-shaped farming terraces stepped down the hill to the wash below. More than twenty of these giant steps guarded each side of the wash—as did two square stone watchtowers, useful, no doubt, over many centuries of warfare. Each terrace was held in place by a stone retaining wall four to six feet high on the downhill side.

Lt. Fabayo laid it out: Team Monti and the lead platoon of Askars would walk up the wash and enter North Ganjigal. Team Monti would continue east to a water tank at the end of the village to make sure no bad guys came down the trail from Pakistan. When the meeting with the elders was finished, we would walk back down to our vehicles and drive twenty minutes back to Joyce.

"We're walking in?" I asked. "We're not taking our gun trucks?"

The way to get into those two hamlets, it seemed to me, was to drive armor right up the wash between them. A half-dozen Humvees with .50-cal guns could provide protection for the meeting. There didn't seem to be any other way to do it. The mountains made it too hard to flank around and get above the villages.

"No. We're going in at dawn," Fabayo said. "The noise of trucks would alert them. I don't want to lose the element of surprise."

Element of surprise, my ass. I didn't know how ninety noisy

Askars, arriving after a day of cell phone chatter, could have an *element of surprise* walking into a mountain village. Even as a twenty-one-year-old E-4, I could assure you that a ninety-man patrol is incapable of having any sort of *element of surprise*.

Lt. Johnson looked at me, shaking his head to warn me to be quiet. He pointed at the map and pantomimed making notes. I got it. He wanted me to stop critiquing what I couldn't change and come up with the tactics for our lead element.

Thinking the danger lay on the far ridgelines and not closer in, my idea was simple. Because Team Monti was in the lead, we'd be the first to engage. So I'd take point with a 240 machine gun with five hundred rounds. I'd put Dodd Ali and his spit-polished SAW on my flank. I assumed we'd be hit by a few snipers, covered by a PKM. If the 240 couldn't suppress them, Dodd Ali would cover me while I called for artillery.

I saw Capt. William Swenson sitting among us. He was the quiet, long-haired Border Police advisor I knew only by reputation. For ten months, he and his SNCO (senior noncommissioned officer), Sgt. 1st Class Kenneth Westbrook, had been living with the police, driving around in an unarmed Ford Ranger pickup. Swenson joked that they were "an Army of Two."

Swenson was on his third combat tour and had held over a hundred key leader engagements with mountain clans. He popped up in the strangest places. Once, when Lt. Kerr was conducting a patrol into very remote valleys outside Dangam, his soldiers stopped by the compound of Gal Rahman, a border police chief. They were greeted by a lanky, beardless man in a gray man-dress and a flat *pahkohl* hat. It was Swenson. He had been invited to a wedding and had stayed on in the mountains for a week as the chief's guest, despite the news that a "soft American target" had made its way back into Pakistan.

I was glad to see Swenson at the briefing. He was known for calling in artillery fire on the dot. Adjusting artillery in the mountains wasn't easy. So I planned to introduce myself to Swenson and compare coordinates.

Fabayo said helicopters weren't in support of us, but would be diverted if needed. He did say artillery was in support and pointed to the Kilo Echoes, or artillery registration points, marked by six red crosses on the photomap. I watched Swenson check them against his own map.

"Three-070 is the Undo KE, correct?" he said.

"Undo" meant we were pulling out. Swenson was concentrating on how we would get out of that box canyon if things went wrong. He wanted a fire mission to conceal our retreat. Maj. Williams believed 1–32 had assured him that "we could put smoke on the deck for screening." KE 3070 was the registration point for that smoke screen.

"KE 3070 is the Undo," Fabayo agreed.

The briefing hadn't addressed command and control. I assumed Maj. Williams, as the senior American, was in charge. Battalion 1–32 believed Williams was in charge. But Williams believed Maj. Talib, the operations officer of the Afghan battalion, was in command. Which is the craziest thing I've ever heard in my entire life. Talib, who spoke broken English, could not call in fire support. But Talib and Williams would be together, so any confusion about command could be resolved on the spot. If everything went according to plan, the trip to Ganjigal would be a pleasant morning hike on a pleasant fall day.

At one point, Maj. Williams said, "I hope we can be back at Joyce in time for lunch."

. . .

As we left the briefing room, I didn't get that chance to corner Capt. Swenson; 1st Sgt. Garza pulled me and Team Monti aside.

"Gunny Johnson is replacing Meyer on this op," he said.

Gunny Johnson handled logistics on base, doing endless paperwork. He was competent, even-tempered, and obliging. If Team Monti needed gear, he found it and shipped it to us. It was not unusual to rotate men on missions where low-level shooting was likely. Hearing a few rounds crack by once during a nine-month tour wasn't too much to ask. Every Marine wanted to qualify for the Combat Action Ribbon. It would suck to be stuck on Joyce, and never qualify for the CAR.

Plus, I wasn't popular at ETT headquarters on Joyce. Fabayo had told me several times that "our job as advisors was not to fight." Headquarters considered me too headstrong. Maybe so, but on this patrol, we were going into a horseshoe-shaped valley with steep mountains on every side, with no trees or undergrowth for concealment, walking uphill for over a kilometer to reach two hamlets where every house was as hardened as a Normandy pillbox.

"I should be with my team, First Sergeant," I said.

I was Team Monti's tactician and gunner. In the dozen-odd scrapes we'd been in, I had burned through ten thousand rounds. I could clear misfires, coax malfunctioning breeches, and quickly swap out one barrel or one gun for another. I had walked fire onto targets at ranges from two hundred to seven hundred meters. On this patrol, I wanted to walk point in front of Lt. Johnson, not babysit the trucks in the rear. The four of us were a unit now.

Staff Sgt. Kenefick and Lt. Johnson agreed with me, objecting strenuously.

"We need Meyer," Staff Sgt. Kenefick said.

"We're a team, First Sergeant," Lt. Johnson said. "It makes no sense to split us up."

"The decision's been made," 1st Sgt. Garza said. "End of discussion."

I tried to keep calm. I couldn't be mad at Garza, as he wasn't the one who had made the decision. I told myself it was my ego that was hurt. I was just steamed because I'd miss some shooting time. It was no big deal; the insurgents never fought from inside a village. Gunny Johnson deserved to go on a patrol. Still, why jerk me off the team? The ETT head shed at Joyce had pulled me out to shove my nose into it, to make me more of a team player, that sort of thing.

The more I stewed, the more upset I became. The mission brief hadn't been thorough. The ridges around Ganjigal bothered the hell out of me. I couldn't shake a bad, bad feeling.

I sought out Staff Sgt. Juan Rodriguez-Chavez, our motor transport chief. I had known him for five months. He didn't stand on rank and we'd traded stories about growing up on farms. He had grown up on a ranch in Mexico. Having a similar approach to life, Rod and I had become friends.

He was in the eighth grade when his family moved to Texas, where he learned English, played football, earned good grades, and roped cows in rodeos. Our team called him "Hot Rod." He laughed a lot, bragged about how smart his two daughters were, and kept all our vehicles in top condition.

"Rod, this mission is fucked up. If the shit hits the fan," I said, "we're going in. My team's walking point, and they'll get cut off. We have to go in and get them out."

"Dakota," Rod said, "don't put this on Gunny Johnson. I heard him and Staff Sgt. Kenefick talking. They're both upset you're not with them."

"I know, Gunny's a good guy. I'm pissed about the whole setup. If

83

they step in shit, they'll need heavy firepower, and we're back here. We have to be ready to push up that wash."

"Devil Dog," Rod said, "say the word, and I'll do the driving."

Having some sort of contingency plan now, I walked back to the advisor headquarters and briefed Lt. Johnson.

"If things get hairy," I said, "I'm coming in. Rod will drive. Radio your coordinates and get down to the wash. Fucking climb in and we'll haul ass back to the main body."

He stared at me for a second, smiled, and burst out laughing.

"Meyer, you're always thinking how to get into it," he said.

He definitely was relieved. I did the fire planning for our team and then I was suddenly gone. Now I was promising I'd figured out a way to be there. The lieutenant was too good a leader ever to speak badly about anyone. He'd joke around about personality tics, but not in a way that undercut anyone's authority. Still, he didn't try to talk me out of it, or tell me to coordinate with Maj. Williams or Lt. Fabayo. My deal with Rod stayed inside Team Monti, and I took that as a green light. If there was trouble, Rod and I were going in.

The lieutenant and I lay down on the two couches in the advisor's office. I could tell he was feeling better about the patrol because he wasn't brooding or going over his notes. Instead, we talked and laughed about silly stuff. Maybe we had made too much fuss about another KLE.

While we were chatting, Fabayo, dressed in flip-flops, shorts, and a T-shirt, walked into 1–32's tactical operations center to drop off our roster, called an equipment density list. Before a convoy leaves a base, all Social Security numbers and blood types are handed in to the duty officer.

In the TOC, a report about Ganjigal had come in via the brigade Internet. A Special Forces team reported that thirty-two fighters were moving from Pakistan to reinforce Ganjigal. Half an hour later, the video feed from an unmanned aerial vehicle showed a man with a mortar tube on his back entering a known safe house, two kilometers north of Ganjigal village. Ten minutes later, four more men entered the same house.

Fabayo knew nothing of these movements; the TOC at Joyce had not mentioned them. Such sightings at night were frequent, and few turned out to be serious. Even so, one of the observations came with this note: "Their movement is too organized to be locals; they have a point man, security element and overwatch. Locals do not move like this. They are utilizing terrain, stopping under cover and hesitating at all open areas."

In fact, Qari Zia Ur-Rahman, head of the Taliban in Kunar Province, had perfect intelligence a day ahead of our movement. He had thrown away his normal tactics, gathered all the forces he could muster, crossed over from Pakistan, and headed toward Ganjigal. He intended to stand and fight from *inside* the village. Twenty Taliban were already in the village; a fighter named Khadim had fifteen more, and Rahman had another fifteen. A leader named Faqir brought in twenty more and set up in five positions: two on the north side, two on the south side, and one in the middle. At 4:13 A.M., a group of fighters had stopped to pray on a hill two kilometers northeast of Ganjigal. They were seen by an eye in the sky, as were the movements of other men coming our way. Before dawn, they were in place in and around Ganjigal, a village so tough to attack that it had served as a major supply point in the war against the Russians.

Fabayo walked back to the advisor area. Neither Lt. Johnson nor I believed the small task force would roll on time. But we left the wire shortly after three in the morning, ten minutes late, which wasn't bad.

On the way in, we talked about our plans for when we got back to the States. We came up with one super scheme: Lt. Johnson would volunteer to be the officer-in-charge of ROTC at a small college. Staff Sgt. Kenefick would be the senior NCO, handling personnel matters. He'd slip Doc Layton and me in as transfer students. The college might be a surf party school or a ski party school—we went back and forth on that.

Under a bright moon and gentle wind, we rolled the two miles north to the jumping-off point. I was in the turret. Staff Sgt. Kenefick drove; Lt. Johnson sat opposite him in the commander's seat, monitoring the radio. Doc Layton sat behind him. Hafez, sitting behind Staff Sgt. Kenefick, changed our mood.

"Ganjigal is a bad valley," Hafez said. "Very bad valley."

"Stop saying that, Hafez," Staff Sgt. Kenefick said.

Everyone was irritable because the team had been broken up. It felt unlucky.

"Meyer, it's your bad," Johnson said. "If you learned how to kiss ass, or at least not kick people in the ass, you'd be coming with us. But no, that's not your style. So stay behind with the trucks and sip chai. See if we care."

"Sir, don't bust my balls. I'll drive in to get you if your feet get sore."

I reminded them of my plan with Rodriguez-Chavez.

"Hot Rod drives like he's in a rodeo," I said. "He can get up that wash. If shit happens, be ready to move."

We were heading toward Little Big Horn.

Chapter 8

INTO THE VALLEY

With lights off, we drove slowly a mile and a half up the dirt track into the valley—half a league, in British military parlance. From there, it would be that distance again, but on foot.

The jumping-off point was called the ORP, or the objective release point. Our convoy consisted of three passenger trucks, six Ford Ranger pickups with open backs, and four armored Humvees. The soldiers hopped out, leaving the thirteen vehicles parked in a long row on the narrow road. It would be hard to get those vehicles out of the way in a hurry, I thought, and hard to get anyone out for medical help. Not a great place to stop, considering there were plenty of wide spots in the dry riverbed.

"Lieutenant," I said to Lt. Johnson, "if we have an emergency medevac, this will be a cluster fuck."

He took Fabayo aside, and a few minutes later we moved the trucks off the track. While the vehicles were repositioned, Staff Sgt. Kenefick took me aside.

"Make sure you monitor the net," he said. "I want you listening up."

"If the shit hits the fan," I replied, "get down to the wash. We'll pick you up."

The patrol formed up single file. Capt. Kaplan, the intelligence officer, took off separately with a small group to set up an observation post on the southern ridge, to our right. Higher up on the same ridge an Army scout-sniper team had already settled in. A third observation team cut left across the rocky wash to establish a post on the northern ridge, a half-mile away.

Gunny Johnson walked up to join my team. It was still dark, but we could see each other under the stars and moon. He knew how I was feeling. He was carrying our 240. Well, the machine gun wasn't complicated to use. Besides, he'd never have to fire it.

Team Monti and our Afghan platoon—the best of them—set off in the lead. Dodd Ali scrambled by me to take point ahead of Gunny. He grinned and gave me a little wave. When Lt. Johnson walked by, he gave me a fist pump. Hafez, busy adjusting his pair of radios, ignored me.

Terrific, I thought, *everyone's excited to be going in, and I'm stuck in the rear.*

Maj. Williams then joined the column with his Command Group, which included 2nd Lt. Fabayo, First Sgt. Garza, Maj. Talib, and an American reporter I hadn't met. The tactical command party (TCP) was the mobile headquarters for the operation. In this instance, it was a few men on foot. Capt. Swenson and his SNCO, Sgt. Ken Westbrook, walked behind the Command Group. Lights in the village more than a mile uphill to the east were still twinkling from the power of the little hamlet's diesel generator.

The Askars remaining with the trucks lit up cigarettes and drank some water. It was Ramadan, so there'd be no eating or drinking once the sun came up. Most were fairly religious, praying five times a day.

The night before, I had urged them to hydrate by drinking at least five bottles of water. By noon, some would be sucking pebbles to take their minds off their thirst.

Staff Sgt. Rodriguez-Chavez and I sat on the hood of my Humvee, listening as the last gravel crunch of the column's march faded out. A few minutes later, all the lights in the village went out at the same time. Someone had pulled the switch.

Swenson's border police turned to Hafez when the lights went out. "Dushmen!" they said. "We must turn back!"

I listened as Johnson sent a warning over the advisor radio net, while the platoon stopped briefly for morning prayers.

All right, I thought. *Now the Command Party knows there's no surprise. They'll call up the gun trucks.*

"Get ready to roll, Rod," I said.

But no, the patrol proceeded toward the village, with some of the border police drifting back to the rear of the column. They weren't trained or equipped for firefights.

A few minutes later, the advisors climbing to the northern overlook radioed that flashlights were winking on and off in the hills to their east, closer to Ganjigal.

Just before five in the morning, Rod and I heard gravel crunching on the trail: men, women, children, sheep, and goats suddenly hurried by our trucks, heading out of the valley. Pre-dawn always brought the first singsong call to prayer, followed by people scurrying about. This morning, I had heard no high-pitched mullah, and these people were not heading to market, they were running away.

I stood in the middle of the path and blocked the departure of a teenager and a tall, older man with a full beard, wearing the cleanest white man-dress I had ever seen.

"*Salaam,*" I said, placing my right hand over my heart in the tra-

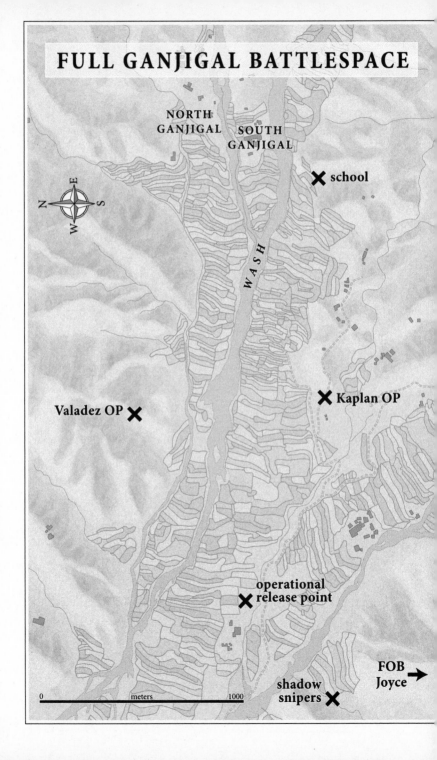

FULL GANJIGAL BATTLESPACE

NORTH
GANJIGAL   SOUTH
GANJIGAL

✖ school

N E
W S

✖ Kaplan OP

Valadez OP ✖

operational
✖ release point

0   meters   1000

shadow
snipers ✖

FOB
Joyce →

WASH

ditional sign of respect toward an elder. *"Singay?"*—what's going on?

Refusing to look at me, the man clicked away at the string of worry beads in his hands. When I tried to shake hands, he ignored me. I was surprised by the open insult. Even when they don't like you, Afghans shake hands, just as Americans do. The teenager smirked. I stepped aside and they strode past.

"What you think, Homey?" Rod asked.

"This sucks," I replied.

Team Monti and the lead platoon had climbed up a series of terrace walls and were entering the outskirts of South Ganjigal as dawn broke. They spread widely apart in the open terrain. Behind them came Majors Talib and Williams, 1st Sgt. Garza, and 2nd Lt. Fabayo. A bit farther back, Swenson was walking with some police, keeping within shouting distance of the others.

As Lt. Johnson approached the first row of houses, he radioed back to Garza that he and Lt. Rhula were heading toward the house of an imam, one of the village elders. Seconds later, an RPG streaked in from the east, followed by a burst from a PKM, the Russian-made machine gun that shoots a hefty 7.62-millimeter cartridge. It started tearing up the ground and the adobe walls. As the men took cover among the terrace walls, more PKM fire came from the northeast, joined by AKs at closer range.

Enemy fighters were crouched inside the houses and below the windows of the schoolhouse on the southern ridge. They were hiding in the alleyways and dug in behind the stone terrace walls to the east. They had a dozen fixed positions and were shooting downhill with the sun behind them.

. . .

I heard the shooting echoing through the valley, ragged at first and subsiding momentarily while magazines were reloaded. Then the volume increased, with mortar and RPG explosions mixed in. The advisor net crackled with voices stepping over each other. Fifteen Marines sharing one frequency were trying to radio their positions and the locations of the enemy.

Bedlam isn't unusual in the first seconds of an attack. When dushmen open fire, they usually rip through several magazines while our guys go flat and scramble for position. Within minutes, the troops normally settle down, the senior man controls radio traffic, the forward observer calls in artillery and helicopters, and the enemy rate of fire slackens. The dushmen then scamper over the ridges and, ten minutes later, quiet descends.

Not this time. I waited for the firing to die down, but it didn't. The staccato chaos of RPG explosions, PKM machine guns, AKs, and M16s increased. I heard the report of a recoilless rifle—basically, a 100-pound, shoulder- or tripod-mounted cannon and a sure sign of a planned ambush, as the dushmen don't lug that over the hills for exercise. Then I heard the crump-crump of their mortar shells.

There was a wild babble of voices on the command radio—advisors yelling at each other to clear the net. No one was taking charge. There was no central command. I was pacing around, frustrated at being out of the fight and not being able to help.

Gunny Chad Lee Miller, approaching his observation position high on the north ridge, saw an enemy strongpoint on a plateau only three hundred meters to his east. The enemy soldiers were launching rounds from a mortar tube while others, inside a bunker there, were firing a DSHKA, a massive Russian antiaircraft gun that sounds like a jackhammer hitting a manhole cover.

Staff Sgt. Guillermo Valadez, another advisor, and six Askars were on a ledge about fifty meters below Miller. They also were facing east, looking directly at the same enemy. Soon both ridgelines were sparkling with fire, as the Askars and dushmen engaged each other with rocket-propelled grenades. Smoke and shrapnel filled the air.

Across the narrow valley on the south ridge, Capt. Ray Kaplan had trudged up to his observation position, winded by the steep climb and amazed by the stamina of Cpl. Steven Norman, a slight but tough Marine lugging a 240 machine gun and several belts of ammo.

Seconds after the ambush began, they were pinned down by PKM fire from the east. Cpl. Norman set up his gun and returned fire, killing the enemy gunner.

The first instinct of the Askars with Kaplan was to run downhill into the valley. Kaplan shouted them back into position.

It was a good thing, because a swarm of dushmen were maneuvering up the hill to overrun them.

Kaplan watched as one dushmen got to his feet to make a rush. Cpl. Norman stitched him squarely and he tumbled downhill. That knocked some enthusiasm out of the others. Kaplan seized the moment, ordering his Askars to spread out and find cover, facing northeast, the direction of the main ground assault. For the next hour, the Askars, Kaplan, and Cpl. Norman would duel with PKM and AK gunners.

Kaplan made his men shift their positions constantly so the dushmen couldn't zero in. He carried Viper binoculars with a laser that measured the distance and azimuth to a target. Before he could get the reading to call in, a bullet smashed through the binoculars. He was all right, but he couldn't call in help from the artillery with any precision.

Enemy fire from the east was swelling like a thunderstorm. RPGs and mortars shells were dropping in, with machine guns delivering accurate fires from the north and south ridgelines. Swenson, marooned out on the terraces below the village, ducked behind a stone wall. He had marked nine artillery registration points on his map; each consisted of a number preceded by the letters KE. It wasn't Swenson's job to act as the forward observer and to call in fire, but he responded automatically.

"This is Highlander 6!" he yelled over the din. "Forward line of troops pinned down at X-Ray Delta 96873 51568. Heavy enemy fire. Request immediate suppression. Fire Kilo Echo 3070. Will adjust."

The southern ridgeline was so high that Swenson's radio couldn't reach the operations center at Joyce, only two miles away. Kaplan, recovering from a bullet into his binoculars, tried to relay the message from his higher perch, but portions of it were garbled. Higher up on the ridge, Staff Sgt. Thomas Summers of the Army scout-sniper team, Shadow 4, finally relayed the message to the TOC.

"Fire KE 3070," Sgt. Summers said. "I will relay adjustments."

I heard the radio command. KE 3070 was the "Undo" fire mission, signaling a withdrawal. Swenson hadn't wasted any time. Once the smoke shells started landing, I assumed Team Monti would pull back. I knew what Rod and I had to do when that happened. That was obvious.

Chapter 9

PARALYSIS

"What you think, man?" Rod said.

"If the dushmen cut around the rear," I said, "and close the back door, they'll catch our people in a fire sack. This is deep shit. They gotta get out of there."

The way to break up an ambush is to hammer it with heavy fire. The Humvee gave us armor, mobility, and a heavy gun. We could roll in and bring Team Monti back to the location of the Command Group. I grabbed the radio and called Fox 3—Lt. Fabayo. No reply. I tried Fox 6—Williams—and then Fox 9—1st Sgt. Garza. No one replied. I was calling for permission to enter the valley, asking for it from anyone who would answer.

Finally, Fox 7—Valadez, up on the northern ridge—answered on the net.

"Fox 3-3, your requests to enter the valley are denied. Fox 9 says you are to stay at your present location."

It made no sense. On my truck was mounted the Mark 19 belt-fed

40-millimeter grenade launcher. Fearsome. It spat out explosive shells as big as a man's fist.

I put down the handset and sat there, listening as a dozen advisors tried to talk over a single radio channel. It was sheer bedlam.

"This is bullshit, Rod."

I rechecked the ammo belt on the Mark 19. Rod sat in the driver's seat.

"You ready, Rod?"

"Give it a few more minutes, Meyer. You'll fry for this," he said.

He was right. I'd get sent home for disobeying a direct order. There was no question in my mind about that. I was already on thin ice with Garza, Fabayo, and Williams. So I sat there, frustrated, listening to the shooting, flexing my hands on the grips of the Mark 19 and breathing hard. I tried to calm down. Maybe the battle sounded worse on the radio than it really was. *Son of a bitch!*

Inside the tactical operations center at Joyce, Capt. Aaron Harting was the senior officer on duty from midnight to eight in the morning—the battle captain. He had been in Afghanistan for eight months but had rarely controlled fires, and certainly none like this one.

His desk was behind a low railing at the south end of the large, square white plywood room. A big electronic map and several video monitors—the eyes in the sky and other sources—were mounted on the north wall. A forest of electronic green boxes and flat-screen monitors were jammed in. Rough plywood shelves held three-ring binders; weapons leaned in plywood stands. Flip-chart easels and chalkboards and whiteboards, water bottles, an electronic coffee-maker, foam cups, bundles of cables going through holes in the walls, paper topo maps taped to walls, exposed air ducts, digital wall clocks with local time and Zulu (Greenwich Mean) time, and soldiers with short haircuts and camo clothing filled all the visual space. Between the electronic map wall and Harting was a long desk with computer screens and radios manned by the half-dozen or more sergeants who daily tracked unit locations and fire missions.

As artillery stood by at Joyce and at Asadabad, a few miles away, Harting asked for more and more information from the men on the long table: Who was requesting the fire missions, was it Shadow 4, Highlander 5 (Swenson), or Fox 3 (Fabayo)? What had they heard from Fox 6—Maj. Williams? Who was presently in charge, the Marine advisors or the Afghan Army? Did the ground commander know where all his troops were? Had they double-checked the grids of the KEs?

He asked question after question.

In the valley, Swenson dodged his way forward one hundred meters to link up with Fabayo, who was calling artillery in on KE-3345, near an enemy machine-gun location, four hundred meters to the east.

At Joyce, 120-millimeter mortars were fired fifteen minutes after Fabayo requested. The first shell, though, struck within fifty meters of the enemy position. The next flurry of shells was on target. That would be the only effective fire mission of the entire day.

The patrol was now in deep trouble. The ridgelines on the horseshoe around them were a tangle of rocky outcroppings and shallow caves. Enemy machine guns, three hundred to six hundred meters east of the patrol, were nestled into snug crevices, far enough back to conceal gun flashes, with angles of fire that crisscrossed the valley. The only cover was the retaining walls of the farm terraces on either side of the wash.

The TOC had recorded Swenson's first request for fire—the "Undo KE"—at 0537. Eventually that request was sent via computer to the 155-millimeter artillery battery at Asadabad, about four miles away. A well-trained artillery battery has shells in the air less than three minutes after a call for fire. It wasn't until twenty-three minutes later that the guns at "A-Bad" fired the mission.

Fabayo grew infuriated by the lack of support. Shifting to another KE, he heard the shells hit in a draw. He made three more adjustments, but hitting a hidden target somewhere on the uneven side of a cliff requires long practice and a prodigious number of shells—and time, which they didn't have. The machine guns kept firing.

Lt. Johnson and the rest of Team Monti had taken cover in a house on the edge of South Ganjigal, while the Askars caught in the open wash scrambled for cover. The enemy above them worked their way around the edges of the valley. Shooting downhill, the Taliban machine-gunners tracked in on one Askar, then another, then another. It was a killing ground.

Swenson, still with Fabayo, plotted another fire mission. They called artillery on KE-3365, a spot above and to the right of South Ganjigal where the enemy's heavy guns were firing. Swenson and Fabayo had identified three enemy machine-gun positions, if they could just get some shells to land on them.

A few meters in front of the two men, an Askar screamed and crawled away, seriously wounded. Two other Askars ran by. Behind them, another yelled, dropped his M16, and limped down the draw. Fire was coming from three directions, kicking up spurts of dust around the two.

They're all over the place, Swenson was thinking to himself. *I may not make it out of here.*

When he wasn't on the radio, Swenson was pointing out shooters to Fabayo, who shot at them with his M4. A few meters behind them, Maj. Williams and 1st Sgt. Garza were popping up and down, trying to provide covering fire, but the patrol was grossly overmatched. The enemy gunners were dialed in, and were delivering ten aimed bullets for every wild shot our guys were throwing back at them. Fabayo sensed that the angle of enemy fire was shifting to the southeast, a sure indication that they were being flanked—soon to be surrounded.

The Afghan operations officer kept asking Maj. Williams what he was going to do. For his part, Williams was hoping that air would arrive any minute to suppress the enemy gunners. The fiction that the Afghans were in charge had fallen apart.

Swenson wasn't waiting for the majors to decide who was in command. He shouted at his police to move farther south to prevent being encircled. Within minutes, however, the police were pinned down and stopped returning fire. Not fighting back is the worst mistake you can make in a firefight. Men instinctively duck when rounds are zipping over their heads. Most firefights are standoff affairs. Each side tests and probes the other, backing off when meeting resistance. Few men press home an assault in the face of return fire.

But if you hunker down and don't shoot back, you will surely die. The other side gains confidence and rushes forward. In the frenzy of combat, soldiers act like sharks. They sense weakness and circle in, picking off the wounded and the defenseless. Slowly the dushmen were closing in from both sides of the wash.

Kaplan, up on the ridge, passed Swenson's fire requests to Shadow 4, the Army scout-snipers up higher on the ridge, at least seven times.

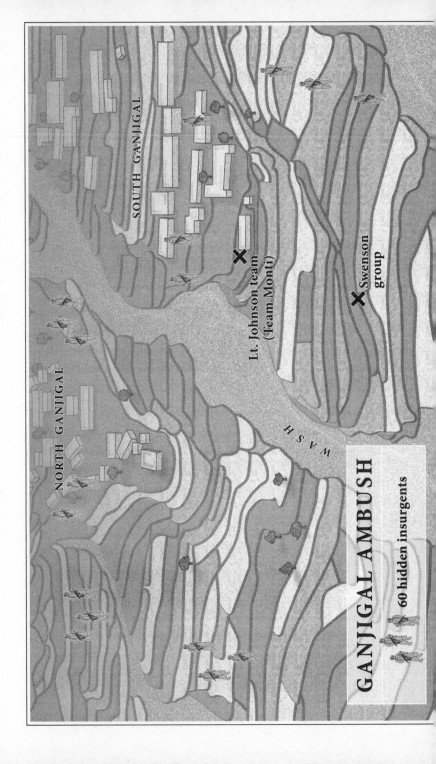

Sgt. Summers at Shadow 4 kept assuring Kaplan that the fire missions were getting through, but . . .

"The TOC won't clear the missions," Kaplan radioed to Swenson. "The fucks won't shoot the arty."

Swenson had identified enemy positions at four grid positions. There are two basic ways of calling in artillery. You can give the grid coordinates of the target or the KE number for a grid, and adjust after the initial round. Or you can give your own location and a compass bearing and distance to the target. This second technique, called a polar mission, provides the guns with the locations of both the friendly observer and the target.

"Tell the TOC I'll send it polar," Swenson radioed to Kaplan. "It's on me! Give them my initials. I'm making the decision, not them!"

Assuming accurate fire—the U.S. mortars were less than two miles away—the only target endangered by the polar plot was the enemy. By sending his initials, Swenson was taking full responsibility. If anything went wrong—if a friendly soldier or a civilian were hit—the burden rested squarely on Swenson, not with the TOC in the rear.

The TOC responded to the polar request by asking again for information impossible to provide. Where were all the friendly troops? What was the forward line of trace of friendly units? Was everyone accounted for? Were any civilians endangered?

It was after 6 A.M. The patrol was half an hour into a losing fight. No one had an account of the locations or the casualties among the sixty Askars scattered in the terraces and the wash.

"KE 3365, Hill 1458," Kaplan told Shadow, the relay team above him. "Tell the TOC that's critical. I repeat, critical. We have advisors pinned down."

Shadow 4 on the southern ridge had eyes on an enemy mortar

team to the south and called in a polar mission. The TOC denied Shadow's fire mission. Furious, Sgt. Summers at Shadow 4 pressed back against the TOC.

"The main element is being hit from the north, east, and south," he said. "All elements are engaged. I repeat, all elements are heavily engaged. We need fire missions now."

The NCOs inside the TOC were doing their job, and the artillery and mortar crews wanted to oblige. Yet it seemed to Sgt. Summers that every time he relayed a fire mission, the TOC asked him "twenty questions." A second string was running the show there, and not well.

Despite repeated requests for half an hour, Fabayo had seen no more than four or five effective rounds.

Not every gun remained silent. Somehow the sergeants in the TOC, despite the indecision of their officers, communicated the urgency to the soldiers firing the 120-millimeter mortars outside at Joyce. The mortars responded to KE 3365 with an eight-round "splash"—with shells on target—inside ten minutes.

Those few shells, however, were not nearly enough. At the Joyce TOC, the fire mission requests were cascading in every four minutes. Most were ignored or given a meager response. In firefights, it's not unusual for two hundred to two thousand artillery shells to be fired. Over the course of the first hour of the battle at Ganjigal, when men lay trapped and dying, the TOC at Joyce allowed only twenty-one artillery shells to be fired.

HIGH COMMAND

Since World War II, forward observers had received artillery fire under the rule of "silence is consent." When an observer called for fire, the mission went by radio to the operations center and to the guns. Silence by the ops center constituted consent for the guns to fire.

In the twenty-first century, with computers making instant firing calculations, within two minutes shells should be hitting the target. But beginning about 2006, sergeants and lieutenants on the front lines were trusted less. The high command believed the grunts were too quick to call in fires that endangered civilians, resulting in an embittered population that supported the insurgency. The solution was to apply a strict new rule.

Two months before Ganjigal, Gen. Stanley McChrystal, the senior commander in Afghanistan, issued a directive that forbade the use of artillery against or near any structure "likely to contain civilians" unless "the next higher headquarters commander has approved." That ended "silence is consent." The high command had shifted decision-making from the battlefield to the staff. Swenson was not trusted to make the hard decisions. Instead, officers in the TOC, with a confused idea of the battlefield, had to decide whether to honor his requests for fire.

Major Peter Granger, the senior officer in the Joyce TOC, later said, "Without knowledge of the exact whereabouts of friendly forces, I did not feel it was worth the risk to clear the fires. That was coupled with a lack of SA [situational awareness] in regards to the disposition of civilians in the area." For the record, I believe this is total bullshit.

The officers in the TOC could see on the map that the fire missions were being called in close to the farming compounds; those officers could not see the friendly troops who were dying. That's the problem—guys like that sit back and worry about protecting their rank more than taking risks and supporting the troops. Even worse, at the end of the day the troops not getting the support go home and have to deal with losing their friends while the officers get promoted and never have to see the results of their decisions up close.

Twenty minutes into the fight, knowing that no artillery support was coming, Swenson was now calling for helicopter support. Once those gunships arrived with their heat-seeking thermal sights, the insurgents typically broke contact or hid inside houses. Swenson called for helicopters, or CCA—close combat aviation. He also asked for fixed-wing attack aircraft, or CAS—close air support.

Again, Shadow 4 relayed the message to Joyce.

"Highlander 5," Sgt. Summers radioed to Swenson, "be advised the TOC says CCA will be at your pos in fifteen mikes [minutes]."

Fifteen minutes is a very, very long time when machine guns, rifles, RPGs, and mortars are firing at you. The fifteen minutes passed without any helicopters. Sgt. Summers kept requesting air. Down in the wash, Swenson was effectively in charge. Everyone was trying to talk to him, asking for guidance. Sgt. Summers kept telling him that the TOC was requesting trivial data, such as battle roster numbers and the last four Social Security digits of each American in the valley. For Swenson, it felt like asking for money from a bank where he didn't have an account.

I could finally hear the thumping echo of the heavy 155-millimeter shells exploding in the upper valley. This had to be KE 3070, the KE Undo, that Swenson had called for twenty-three minutes earlier. At last, my team would be concealed by smoke. Then I heard Swenson saying he had asked for smoke, not high explosives. Negative, came the relayed reply from Joyce—no smoke rounds available. None, in fact, anywhere in theater.

Fox 3–1—Lt. Johnson—finally came up on the radio.

"We're pinned down in a house," he said. "Receiving accurate fire from the next house. We have to get out of here."

He was cut off by others pushing to use the same frequency. Three or four advisors were trying to talk, stepping on each other. I could hear the strain in their voices, the lack of crisp orders, the frantic yelling of men who were pinned down.

A few minutes later, Fox 3–2—Staff Sgt. Kenefick—tried to pass his location on the grid to Fabayo.

"I can't shoot back," Aaron said, "because I'm pinned down. They're shootin' at me from the house, and it's so close. Grid . . ."

"Three-2, this is 3-3," I radioed to Staff Sgt. Kenefick. "Repeat your grid. Repeat grid."

Nothing after that but static and garbled voices. That broke it for me. I had promised my team I would be there. As far as I was concerned, my command element wasn't in command.

Chapter 10

LOST

Until I heard those radio calls, I assumed Team Monti was on its way out. I figured things would unscrew themselves, that Maj. Williams would take charge and artillery and helicopters would roll in, allowing my team to link up with the Command Group. The fight had been raging for over half an hour.

Up on the north lookout, Gunny Miller was directing his RPG gunner in a duel with the Russian DSHKA antiaircraft gun. Several feet below him, Staff Sgt. Valadez—Fox 7—had been listening to my shouts over the radio. He relayed my message to Fabayo. Overwhelmed with his own problems, Fabayo told Valadez to stay off the net.

"Fox 3–3, this is Fox 7," Valadez radioed to me. "Fox 3–2 [Staff Sgt. Kenefick] told me he's in a house. I don't have a grid. You're supposed to stay where you are."

Twice I had heard Shadow say that air would be on station in fifteen minutes. Nothing had happened. How long do you do nothing while your friends are fighting for their lives?

"Fox 7, this is 3–3. Sitting here is stupid. We're going in."

Rod and I were on the net with Valadez. There was no dispute among us. It was about 0600—time to move. I was the vehicle commander, so the fault lay with me for disobeying orders if I arrived in the valley and discovered that the Command Group had the situation under control. I knew there was a good chance I'd be sent back to the States in disgrace. When I shouted to the Askars to follow us, they looked confused. Up on the north outpost, Valadez grabbed a senior Afghan sergeant. The sergeant radioed to the Afghan drivers clustered around our truck, urging them in Pashto to follow me.

Mortar shells were falling a football field away, to our west. The enemy knew our trucks were somewhere on the path but uncertain just where. The explosions made the Askars jumpy. Just the same, some of them jumped into the two Humvees and roared into position behind us.

"Rod, let's go," I said. He put it in gear.

We headed slowly east on the narrow path that twisted among the uneven farming terraces, looking for a trail down to the wash off to our left. We were driving blind toward the sound of the guns. We hadn't gone two hundred meters when PKM rounds started striking around us. They were coming from a ridge to our east, near Capt. Kaplan's observation post.

For a minute, I was confused. There was a torrent of firing a kilometer to our northeast, where the command group was pinned down. But we hadn't yet reached the wash, off to our left. So why were we under fire?

Then the light clicked on. I was too accustomed to the dushmen being on the defense, shooting and falling back. These pricks were on the offense, with separate packs moving west along the ridges on both sides of us. One group had skirted around Kaplan's strong point.

Shooting from higher ground, our truck looked to them like easy prey.

I pivoted the Mark 19 and looked for muzzle flashes. None. The dushmen weren't firing from exposed positions along the lip of the ridges; they were hunkering back in fixed positions. I watched for dust curls. Water was so scarce that the dushmen usually didn't wet down the ground in front of the guns to help conceal their positions. When I saw a few wisps about five hundred meters away, I pumped out three-round bursts of explosive 40-millimeter shells, using the quick flashes of their detonations to adjust my aim. The PKM, however, continued shooting.

We drove east another hundred meters when the Mark 19 jammed. I hadn't fired more than 30 bursts and I always kept a clean, well-oiled gun. I worked the breach but the shell refused to eject, as if it had been welded into place. I switched to the 240 machine gun I kept in the turret as a backup. It wasn't attached, so every time we hit a rut or bounced over a rock, which was about constantly, I'd throw a burst of fire in some crazy direction.

"Rod, I need a stable gun," I called down the turret to him. "We gotta go back and get another truck."

Rod had to move back and forth five or six times to turn us around, while I waved at the Afghan Humvees to follow us—I didn't want them going in alone, and I didn't want them parked in the line of fire. Back at the operational release point, we ran to another truck, threw extra cans of ammo into the back, and I climbed up into the turret behind a fresh .50-cal.

By that time, several Askars were stumbling out of the battlefield, some bleeding, a few without their rifles, all exhausted.

"Where Americani?" I yelled. "Dost? Dost?"

The Askars pointed up toward the village.

Again we started forward, passing more exhausted Askars as I threw them a few bottles of water. From his northern outpost, Valadez could see our truck.

"Fox 7, this is 3–3," I radioed to Valadez, "we're lost down here. I don't know how to get up to the village.

"Fox 3–3, roll to the Monti net," Valadez said. "I'll guide you in."

I switched to the alternative frequency and looked up at the huge ridge to my left.

"Fox 7, I have no idea where you are," I radioed. "I can't follow your directions."

Valadez, with the enemy shooting at him, draped a bright orange air panel over a big rock. When he said "go right" or "go left," I used the panel to orient myself and shout the direction down to Rod. About 150 meters down the trace, Valadez told me to take a sharp turn to the left.

We went down into a draw. When we popped out the other side, a volley of RPGs hit us, one exploding so close to our left side that Miller, who was on the ledge above Valadez, thought we had been hit dead center.

"Fox 3–3," he radioed to me, "you have enemy at your nine o'clock, driver's side."

That dushmen pack off to our east had been waiting for us. We took some PKM bursts, followed by a few mortar shells to our left front. I blindly fired the .50-cal while Rod kept the truck moving forward. We passed a group of Askars hiding in a ditch who waved frantically at me.

"Rod, hold up!"

Five Askars made a mad dash for the truck. Three piled into the backseats, while two others ran around to the rear, popped open the trunk, and crawled in. Once the doors were shut, Rod turned the truck around and we bounced back up the track. He pulled in behind a small rise that gave shelter from direct fire.

"Drop them off?" Rod shouted.

"Good a place as any!"

When we stopped, the Askars refused to get out. I screamed at them and they tumbled out. I hopped down, closed the trunk, and rearranged the ammo boxes on the rear seats so I could get at them easier in the fight ahead. Rod turned us around and again we headed east. Toward the wash and the heavy fight, fifty or sixty Askars were trapped in the valley, along with my friends. The Afghan Humvees didn't seem to be behind us anymore. Somewhere behind us was a U.S. Army platoon. It seemed to me to be time for them to make a move. They were the quick-reaction force, our insurance policy.

Valadez was on the radio, arguing with Dog 3–6, the quick-reaction Army platoon leader.

"Dog 3–6, this is Fox 7," Valadez radioed. "You need to get in there, man. Fox 3–3's to your front in a Humvee. Drive east until you link up with him."

"Fox 7, this is Dog 3–6," the lieutenant said. "Our vehicles are too big for the mission."

We were driving on a footpath that was barely wide enough for our Humvee. Valadez came up with an alternative.

"Dog 3–6, this is Fox 7," Valadez radioed. "I understand. Drive forward until you reach the Afghan vehicles. Use them to get into the fight. There are people out there dying!"

The platoon leader said he had to wait for clearance from the TOC at Joyce. Right.

. . .

I heard Swenson again asking for air, as he had been doing for about forty-five minutes. Again, the TOC was promising it would arrive in "fifteen mikes." I later learned that inside the TOC, Staff Sgt. Lantz had grabbed a radio and, ignoring the battle captain, called the ops center at Jalalabad Air Base, seventeen miles to the south.

"We have a bad TIC (troops in contact) in Ganjigal," Lantz said. "Those guys need your help right away."

The squadron had helicopters in the air supporting an operation north of Ganjigal. The squadron ops chief agreed to re-task the birds immediately. Over the radio net, the pilots heard the request and flew south. Lantz had gone out of channels, and no written request had been sent via the official computer net. Lantz didn't care; help was at last on the way.

Inside the TOC at Joyce, Tech Sgt. Matzke, the Air Force NCO in charge of air support, demanded that the battle captain authorize fixed-wing close air support in addition to helicopters. Harting, the battle captain, hesitated, not saying yes or no, letting the request dangle in the air.

Five minutes later, the helicopter ops center called back, saying re-tasking of the birds had been canceled because Lantz had not called his own brigade headquarters to ask permission and because another mission north of Ganjigal was of "higher priority."

The refusal was too much for Shadow 4 up on the southern ridge. Sgt. Summers came back on the net, shouting that Ganjigal was "a heavy TIC," meaning that Swenson's requests should take priority and that the helicopters should be re-tasked immediately. Capt. Harting ignored Shadow's plea and did not immediately call his brigade headquarters to demand air support.

Capt. Kaplan heard that exchange and passed the bad news to Swenson.

"We are not getting any air," Kaplan radioed. "They said it was unavailable."

Down in the dirt where bullets were dusting up the ground around him, Swenson burst out laughing at how ridiculous the situation was. Harting had already acknowledged an estimate from the Shadow observation post that "thirty to sixty AAF" (Anti-Afghan Forces) were attacking. Ten minutes later, the TOC again received requests from Shadow for smoke in order to break contact. The requests were "denied twice due to proximity of structures." The TOC assessed the enemy to number up to sixty—and wouldn't authorize fire support.

Swenson and Fabayo sat stunned.

Lt. Johnson again contacted Fabayo on the radio.

"You need to bound back to us," Fabayo said. "We have to fall back."

"We're pinned," Johnson said. "If we leave, we'll get shot. Get us smoke to get out of here."

Swenson knew there was no smoke coming, so he called for white phosphorus rounds.

"We need Willie Peter," Swenson radioed to the TOC at Joyce.

White phosphorus is a sticky, gummy substance that burns intensely. It throws off a cloud of thick white smoke and is routinely used to conceal the movement of troops. Swenson wanted the Willie Peter to explode along the edge of the village. That way, the enemy machine-gunners would be shooting into a fog bank, permitting Team Monti to fall back to Swenson's position on the lower steps of the terrace.

White phosphorus is permitted by the UN Convention governing the rules of war. But during the Fallujah battle in Iraq in 2004, charges that Willie Peter had burned civilians created an uproar in the press. The TOC at Joyce denied Swenson's request, explaining that the village was too close.

More than an hour into the fight, the situation was as follows: Team Monti was trapped in a house; the U.S. and Afghan commanders were pinned down by shooters closing in on them from three sides; the north and south observation posts were under fire; the Askars were caught in the open with nowhere to hide; Rod and I hadn't reached the wash; the 1–32 quick-reaction platoon was not quick-reacting; the TOC at Joyce was paralyzed, preventing artillery support; and the helicopter gunships had not arrived.

Maj. Peter Granger, the executive officer now in command of the battalion while the highly competent Lt. Col. Mark O'Donnell was on leave, kept a cot in his office outside the TOC. Whenever he walked into the TOC, he was in charge as the senior man. But his occasional appearances only reinforced Capt. Harting's hesitancy.

"They [the Marine advisors and Afghan officers] didn't know where all their soldiers were," Granger said later. "They didn't know if they'd be calling fire on their own. They didn't have SA [situational awareness]."

I could hear Swenson's angry voice on the radio. How the hell was he to know where everyone was? That wasn't the point. He knew where the machine guns were—in the hills around the village. Some from the lead platoon had run by him, streaming blood and shouting, some without their helmets or rifles. As he grabbed at two of them, bullets chipped the stones at his feet. All three flopped down as rounds cracked overhead.

Some Askars, pinned down, weren't returning fire. Dushmen with

AKs were sneaking forward on the far sides of the terrace walls, picking off Afghan soldiers lying helpless on the ground. The Askars were targets, waiting to be hit in the beaten zone.

Swenson wanted a massive artillery barrage. Because the dushmen didn't have overhead cover, artillery airbursts would send millions of lancets racing down toward them. Hundreds of shells had to shake the mountains and roll thunder down the valley. The dushmen were zealots, but they weren't crazy. Once artillery began exploding overhead, gunmen with AKs wouldn't get up and run forward in the open. Each salvo of four artillery shells exploded with enough blast and red-hot shrapnel to blanket an entire football field.

Yet the TOC refused to fire at Ganjigal, only a few miles from Camp Joyce. Unleashing a barrage in your own backyard wouldn't win any applause at higher headquarters. The directive from the high command was clear: do not employ "air-to-ground or indirect fires against residential compounds, defined as any structure or building known or likely to contain civilians, unless the ground force commander has verified that no civilians are present."

After the fight had raged for over an hour, the TOC at Joyce finally directed Dog Platoon to prepare to move forward to the valley as "a potential QRF [quick-reaction force]." The platoon leader, Lt. Bielski, replied that he had not been given a grid location for a link-up with the force in the valley, and he hadn't been told how far he was to advance. Again, there was hesitation.

With Dog Platoon unwilling to help, Maj. Williams handed his cell phone to his interpreter, asking him to call for an Afghan quick-reaction force. Soon Afghan Humvees were leaving Camp Joyce—without any Americans from 1–32 joining them.

Fabayo began talking to Johnson about an egress route, when he saw friendly mortar rounds landing on KE 3365.

First Sgt. Garza watched the eight 120-millimeter shells detonate with no effect on the enemy rate of fire. Worse, many of the Askars were no longer returning fire. Some had emptied their magazines; others, not accustomed to the new M16s, had experienced jams and thrown away their rifles.

The Command Group was taking fire from three sides: from the village to their front, from the ridges to the south, and from the terraces to the north.

Lt. Johnson came back on the net, again requesting smoke "to conceal their movement." I heard him give a grid, exactly where he wanted the shells to land. He was calm on the radio. Shadow, the Army outpost on the southern ridge, replied that the TOC at Joyce said the fire mission was too close to the village.

"Too close to the village?" Lt. Johnson said. "If you don't give me these rounds right now, I'm gonna die."

"Try your best," Shadow replied, knowing the TOC wouldn't fire.

Try your best? From the tone of Shadow's voice, I knew he was on the verge of complete rage. He wanted to strangle the officers in the TOC at Joyce. I felt the same way. This couldn't be happening. We were on the same side. We weren't Marines or soldiers; we weren't Americans or Askars. We were one lone group fighting desperately to stay alive. The villagers weren't our friends. This was war, and my team was on the verge of dying. Whose side was the TOC on?

Radio call after call, Swenson kept requesting smoke. Finally, around 0630 the TOC at Joyce permitted four white phosphorus rounds to be fired into the southeast backside of the village, too far away to conceal my team. Those were the last rounds fired during the battle.

At about 0640, the TOC at Joyce forbade any more artillery support, citing garbled communications, incomplete calls for fire procedures, and a lack of situational awareness on the part of those trapped in the valley.

The enemy fire was holding steady, with occasional mortar rounds and RPGs mixed in with the PKM machine guns and the heavy DSHKA. The angle of the fire had shifted southeast, indicating to Fabayo that the Command Group was being cut off.

After an hour with no helicopter gunships or artillery response, the villagers joined the winning side. Fabayo sensed that more and more men were shooting at him from inside the town. Lying behind a dirt mound, he saw flashes coming from a house on a hill to his right. Fabayo blasted the window of the mud house and the fire from that spot ceased. A woman in a red and purple dress was carrying ammunition from one house to the next. Swenson saw another woman stacking rocks to make a fighting position; he didn't shoot at her.

With the villagers spontaneously contributing a base of fire from the shelter of their houses, the hard-core enemy fighters seized the opportunity to sneak behind the terrace walls to cut off the Command Group. Fabayo saw that the far ambush was becoming a near ambush.

The Command Group had to pull back. Swenson and Fabayo provided covering fire as Maj. Williams and 1st Sgt. Garza fell back, with rounds hitting at their feet. The reporter who was with them chose not to risk the run. He remained on the ground, with his face in the dirt. Williams and Garza were running in the open with machine-gun rounds striking in front of them. Garza sprawled flat just in time to avoid a burst right over his head. Next, an RPG exploded near him, throwing him to the ground. Dazed, he struggled up. Williams grabbed Garza and pulled him behind a terrace wall.

Lt. Johnson and Team Monti were still holed up in a house as the Command Group fell back to avoid being surrounded.

As we moved forward for the third time, the TOC had finally ordered the Army platoon—Dog 3–2—to move forward. They pulled in behind us, with the platoon leader in a Humvee with an anti-tank TOW missile on the roof. The TOW made no sense to me, but the truck was equipped with a 240 machine gun. Behind him were twenty U.S. soldiers in four heavily armored vehicles.

"You rolling with me, Lieutenant?"

I was confirming what I took for granted.

"I'll scout the route first, before I bring my platoon in. The terrain may be too tough."

He refused to put his soldiers into the Afghan vehicles. I could understand that.

"Okay. I go first," I said. "You cover our six. The Afghans will be behind you."

I waved to the Afghans standing beside their trucks.

"Burayam! Let's go!" I said.

We headed down the trace, with Valadez giving us directions. It was about 0645. As we bounced forward, I heard Team Monti again come up on the radio.

"We're under fire," Lt. Johnson said. "We're surrounded!"

· · ·

117

The Command Group had now fallen back into the terraces below North Ganjigal. They were spread out, but close enough to shout back and forth. Lt. Fabayo saw our Humvee a few hundred meters to the west, well behind his forward position. He urged the Askars huddled around him not to get up and run toward us. He pointed to a dead Askar nearby.

"If you stand up," he shouted, "that's going to happen to you. You got to keep calm."

Swenson's interpreter, Shafi, was listening on his handheld when an insurgent leader came up on the border police radio net. The insurgent had either taken the handheld from a dead policeman or had bought it in the market. The police, the Askars, and the Taliban all used cheap, commercial handhelds and often hurled insults at one another.

"The Russians made the same mistake coming here," the insurgent said in Pashto. "The elders invited you in; I decide if you leave. You must surrender."

Shafi yelled the message across to Swenson, who dismissed the taunts as crazy talk. Fabayo was lying nearby behind a small mound of dirt to avoid the grazing fire of a machine gun. He heard some shouts in Pashto, something about giving up. He glanced up to see what he thought were four Askars in Kevlar helmets, their gear askew, coming around the side of a terrace. He yelled at them to get down.

But the soldier in the lead had a beard, a green chest rig, an armored vest, and cream-colored pants. He was no Askar. When the soldier raised an AK, Fabayo shot him in the chest. Low on ammunition, Fabayo then scrambled over to Williams to get more magazines. The three other dushmen hesitated long enough for Swenson to lock eyes with a man wearing a black helmet. Then the enemy slid back around the corner. Swenson reached into his pack, took out a grenade, lobbed it over the terrace wall, and ducked.

I hope I pulled the cap off the grenade, he thought. *I don't want some kid to find it intact and blow himself up.*

The grenade detonated and the fighters did not reappear. Rahimula, Major Williams' interpreter, was then shot and killed. More dushmen were moving in from the terraces to the south to cut them off. Fabayo took a head count before falling farther back.

"Where's the reporter?" he yelled. "Where's the reporter?"

Swenson thought the reporter was dead. But after about twenty-five minutes, he risked the fire and ran back to the Command Group. Fabayo's M4 had jammed and Swenson, who carried five hundred rounds for his M4, was busy providing suppressive fire for the entire command party. Fabayo checked on the three wounded Askars lying a few feet away. One had been shot again in the back and had died. Fabayo was soaked in so much blood that the notepad in his pocket had crumbled. Off to his left, he saw a bleeding Askar jump down from a higher terrace, screaming for help. Fabayo started to crawl to him when he heard Williams yell, "I'm hit!"

"You okay, Major?" Fabayo shouted.

Williams had been hit in the inside of his left forearm.

"I'm fine," Williams said. "Keep going!"

Fabayo reached the Askar, who had been shot in the lower stomach. As he applied an H bandage, two other Askars straggled over to him. Both Lt. Rhula and his first sergeant had been shot in their thighs. Fabayo cut away their trousers, wrapped the wounds in gauze, and handed them anti-infection pills.

Several meters away, Garza and Sgt. 1st Class Westbrook, Swenson's NCO, were firing steadily.

Fabayo was pinned down by the machine-gun fire when he heard Garza yell, "Sergeant Westbrook's been hit!"

Garza ran over to Westbrook, who, with blood oozing from his neck, was struggling to get to his feet. Rounds were zipping past as the dushmen aimed in to finish him.

"Stay down!" Garza said, looking at the wound. "Stop trying to get up. You'll get shot."

The three wounded Askars crawled to the stone wall holding up the edge of the terrace and dropped down to the next terrace, leaving Fabayo alone. Swenson looked back to see one Askar stand up and take a bullet in the neck.

Garza, out in the wash thirty meters away, yelled for help moving Westbrook out of the line of fire. The reporter rushed out and together they pulled Westbrook back. Fabayo dropped his first-aid bag and sprinted across to Garza, who was holding Westbrook's hand and reassuring him. Westbrook was heavy, and it took the reporter, Garza, and Fabayo pulling together to carry him behind a terrace wall.

A bullet had entered Westbrook's neck near the shoulder blade and ricocheted downward, a dangerous but not fatal wound. Swenson applied Quick Clot powder and a bandage to seal off the bleeding.

The fight had been raging for over ninety minutes and the chain of command throughout Kunar Province was on alert. Procedures for releasing helicopters had been unsnarled, and two OH-58 Kiowas were en route to the valley. At 0715, they contacted Swenson.

"Highlander, this is Pale Horse," the PC (pilot in command) radioed. "What do you need?"

"Pale Horse," Swenson replied, "am under heavy fire from the village and the hills to the east and on both sides. Request immediate suppression while we pull back."

The Kiowa squadron had been in Kunar for ten months. The pilots knew the terrain and enemy habits. They intended to swoop in low in crisscrossing strafing runs, deliberately swerving and cutting back at odd angles. They didn't care whether they hit the dushmen;

they wanted to force them to crouch down and cease firing. The aerial tactics would allow the Command Group to pull back westward down the draw under reduced enemy pressure. The reporter and Garza propped up and carried Westbrook and some of his gear.

As Swenson moved, he called for a medevac. Shadow radioed back that the TOC wanted questions answered before calling for one.

"Is he Army or Marine?" Shadow said.

Swenson cursed; Maj. Williams was more diplomatic.

"This is Fox 6," Williams radioed. "It doesn't matter his service. He's U.S."

There was a pause, then Shadow reluctantly radioed, "Repeat, TOC needs to know if he's Army or Marine. It's in the regulations."

Swenson ignored the request. Fabayo and Swenson unfolded their orange air panels in preparation for a medevac by helicopter. When that drew the attention of the enemy machine-gunners, Swenson ordered everyone to pull back west another two hundred meters. As they were falling back, Williams and Garza were carrying the gear of the wounded and returning fire, while Westbrook, barely conscious, was helped by Fabayo and the reporter. At least twice they had to duck for cover as machine-gun bullets and rocket-propelled grenades impacted behind them and to their right side.

Standing up in the turret, I saw the group of Americans staggering down the wash to our left. Our Humvee was almost clear of the terraces and about to enter the wash when Rod came to a sudden halt. There were big bags of a white powder in the path just ahead. It was the stuff the dushmen use to make roadside bombs. There was no way to go around the bags. We had a cliff wall on our left and a sharp drop-off on the right.

Rod shouted up the turret.

"Looks bad, Homey!"

Chapter 11

INTO THE FIRE

It was standard procedure for the dushmen to place sacks of ammonium nitrate in shallow holes, insert a blasting cap, and run a wire to a flashlight battery. They'd cut the wire and glue each strand to a piece of wood, with the ends almost touching. When a foot or a tire wheel applied pressure, *boom*.

"I don't think they had time to wire them up," I said. I had no way of knowing that for sure, but I wanted to believe it. They might have seen us coming and rigged it in a hurry to cut us off.

"You ready?" Rod said.

He dropped the truck into gear. I hung on to the turret, eyes squeezed shut. I waited to be flung into the sky and wondered if I could do a backflip in the air and land on my feet—not that it would make any difference. I'd be dead, but you have a few funny thoughts in the infinite split seconds of a battle.

We rolled over the bags. There was a slight bump, and we continued driving.

"All right!" Rod yelled.

Ahead of us the trail cut sharply to the left and led down into a gully. Rod hit the accelerator, and we gained speed downhill. I lost sight of Valadez's orange air panel up on the ridge. Then we popped out on the far side of the gully.

I saw Hafez. He was staggering past us, holding up another Askar.

"Stop!" I yelled to Rod.

I climbed down and grabbed Hafez. He had been nicked in the right arm and another bullet had lodged in the armor plate on his back. He was dirty and tired. He drank some water while I bandaged his arm.

"Very bad in there," he said. "All confused."

"Where's Lieutenant Johnson?"

Hafez shook his head.

"We were in a house, heavy shooting," he said. "The lieutenant told me to go first. I knew the way. He'd follow."

He described what happened next: They ran out of the house and across a terrace. They leapt into a trench to catch their breaths before making the next bound. The trench, visible on our photomaps, slashed diagonally, leading uphill toward the schoolhouse occupied by the enemy.

Lt. Johnson said he'd cover Hafez, who helped two wounded Askars hobble downhill. With bullets zinging about him, Hafez ran at a fast clip. He didn't see or hear Lt. Johnson after that.

Hafez and the two wounded Askars joined the Command Group scattered in the terraces beside the wash. He had heard an insurgent leader, whose voice he did not recognize, tell his men to stay off their radios and use their cell phones.

Dushmen were pressing in on the Command Group from both sides, yelling in Pashto to the Askars to surrender. A wounded Askar next to Hafez threw down his M16.

"If you give up," Hafez said, "I'll shoot you. No one surrenders."

At one point, Hafez said Maj. Williams was lying next to him, returning fire. Two dushmen in dirty man-dresses peeked over a terrace wall about thirty feet away and gestured to them to surrender. Hafez clawed at his gear and threw a smoke grenade. They ducked away and didn't reappear.

Hafez left the Command Group to sort itself out and, helping a wounded Askar, was heading west back to the operational release point when I had stopped him.

"I need you to come back in with me. I can't find them without you," I said.

Hafez had recently married. He was wounded and exhausted. He could now go home and have a life.

"If today is my time to die, then I die."

He climbed into the truck next to Rod. After placing my bulging medical bag and ten boxes of ammo on the rear seats, I strapped a handheld radio to the gun turret so I could listen for Lt. Johnson and we moved out again.

"Can you show us a way in?" I said.

Hafez shook his head.

Wounded Askars were straggling by us. One was holding a bloody cloth to his face, another was hobbling on a shredded leg. The exhausted Askars had stopped where the shallow gully and steep terraces gave them protection from direct fire. Some were stretched out on the ground. The spot would serve as our casualty collection point.

Shortly after we headed again down the valley, we bumped into another group of wounded Askars. Rod recognized their first sergeant, who was dripping blood down the right side of his trousers.

He was waving his arms, begging us to stop. Four Askars hobbled over and threw themselves into the backseats, splashing blood all over the place. We drove them back to the collection point. The first sergeant was blubbering, begging us not to go back in. I was a little rough shoving him out of the truck. I was running out of time and patience. Once we dropped them off, we gunned it back down the track.

To our front, the narrow path opened up into a broad wash, layered with rocks the size of bowling balls. The dry riverbed ran straight to Ganjigal, still half a mile onward. On both sides of us lay the terraced hillsides running up to the two halves of the town, one on each side of the wash.

I heard Staff Sgt. Kenefick on the radio.

"Everyone stop talking on the net," he said. "I gotta get a medevac. I need to give a grid. Nine seven . . ."

His transmission broke up. I hastily scribbled the two digits on the side of my turret.

Seconds later, Valadez came up on the net.

"Fox 3–3, this is Fox 7," he said. "From what I see, you better stay in the center of the wash. There are a lot of bad guys on both sides."

That didn't give Rod much room to maneuver. Where we were, the wash wasn't sixty meters wide. Two Kiowas were up in front of us, following Swenson's radio instructions. We were getting to a place where we couldn't turn around, and couldn't dodge and weave as the RPG smoke trails came at us.

"We could get pretty stuck in here!" Rod yelled.

The truck had very little traction and absolutely no cover.

"Then I guess we'll die with them!" I yelled back.

What else could I say? We weren't going back.

Rod shifted into low gear and we bounced forward over the bowling ball–sized boulders. Up ahead, I saw a cloud of yellow smoke—then I saw our Command Group stagger out of it. I recognized Maj. Williams and 1st Sgt. Garza stumbling forward. Some others were supporting a wounded Army soldier. I saw Capt. Swenson yelling orders. I couldn't reach him over the radio, but no words were needed. With a Kiowa overhead, the Command Group was trying to get out of the wash. They included about six Americans and six Afghans—no one from Team Monti. We couldn't fit them all in the vehicle, so we would just have to give them cover while they moved.

"I don't want to shoot blind through that smoke!" I yelled. There might be more of our guys coming through it. We did have to give them cover from their rear, somehow.

"I'll pull around to the other side of the smoke!" Rod yelled back. "Get ready to fire."

He rocked the truck over the rocks and through the foul-smelling smoke until we bobbled into the open on the far side. The volume of incoming fire didn't seem that bad: bullets from two PKM machine guns a good way up the valley and AK rounds from the nearby terraces were cracking past us. I returned fire in the several directions to slow down their rates of fire. When I looked behind me, the smoke had cleared, and the Command Group had made it out of the wash and into the trace leading back to the casualty collection point.

"Let's move up until they see us!" I yelled, meaning my team.

To our right, about four hundred meters away and thirty stories up the slope, was the schoolhouse that was now an enemy machine-gun bunker. Our truck was taking a few whacks from the PKM, but 7.62-millimeter bullets couldn't punch through our three-inch steel.

My .50-caliber rounds couldn't break through the concrete schoolhouse, but we were a moving target and they weren't, and I could suppress their fire whenever I raked their open windows.

From the western edge of North Ganjigal, another PKM was chipping away at us. Its exact location was impossible to spot, because it wasn't firing any tracers. I could see a crevice the gun might be nested in, so I sprayed in that general direction.

To our right on the ridge above the terraces, a third PKM sometimes shot at us. That gun was also engaging Kaplan at our northern outpost. I just didn't have time for that one, so I ignored it.

In South Ganjigal, about four hundred meters ahead, a few women and children were running back and forth among the houses. Below the houses, a few guys without weapons stepped out from behind terrace walls, looked at our truck, and ducked out of sight. Maybe they were farmers with rocks in their heads. In other villages, sometimes civilians had stood gawking while I exchanged fire with dushmen. Insanity.

Once I had a rough idea where the fire was coming from, I shifted my gaze to take a general look around. The fields around us were littered with the bodies of Afghan soldiers, some tucked up against the terrace walls and others lying behind little rocks or in shallow depressions. It looked like the set of a Hollywood war movie. When the director yelled *Action!*, I expected the soldiers to stand up and take their assigned places.

For maybe two or three seconds, I didn't get it. It was surreal, all those bodies just lying there. I couldn't be looking at corpses. They couldn't all be dead. Sure enough, as the truck bounced forward, I'd see an Askar wave his hand slightly or twitch his foot back and forth, signals of life from men too scared to move.

In a firefight, you're shooting blind most of the time. When you hear the first bullets whiffing past your face or the crump of a mortar shell, your body seeks cover—you don't consciously think about it. Your instincts know it's time to be absolutely flat on Mother Earth.

You shoot from the prone position. If you're well trained, you aim at where you think the fire is coming from and squeeze off burst after burst. If you're ill trained, you shoot wild, holding the rifle above your head. Even when you're doing it right, you rarely have a man in your sights. You shoot at an area where your enemy is also lying down, trying to stay out of sight. Once you're flat, your enemy can't see you—unless, like here, he's up above you. That's why you always want the high ground in battle. That's why Ganjigal was hell.

Rod was swerving the Humvee through the rocks, keeping us moving forward while zigzagging. There was a brush of wind past my cheek—a low hum like a bee, which was a round losing velocity and going subsonic. The air was full of static, like listening to a radio in a thunderstorm. A few bullets clinked off our truck, sounding like gravel thrown up by the wheels. We had driven into the middle of a perfect ambush. The contours of the ridges and terraces reminded me of the Roman Colosseum, with the Taliban spectators armed with AKs and our Hummer the only Christian thing moving on the arena floor.

I looked behind us. The Army Humvee with the TOW missile had closed the gap. Its 240 machine gun could cover our rear. Then, and to my astonishment, the TOW truck stopped and began a laborious but determined U-turn. The track was narrow, with ditches on both sides. It took over a dozen back-and-forths for the truck to turn tail and run.

One of the unit's heavy trucks had slipped off the trace near the casualty collection point and rolled slowly over, landing back on its wheels. The four soldiers inside were strapped tightly in their seats and suffered only mild bruises. The lieutenant turned around and left to go see about it.

We were alone again and very exposed. Puffs of dirt from bullets pelted the ground like hailstones; the air was full of cracklings and rumblings, as if an invisible thunderstorm were rolling across the sky.

Only Rod's skill at the wheel was preventing me from being hit again and again. Bullets make different sounds when they pass by you. The cracks of bullets breaking the sound barrier mean they're high, maybe five or ten feet over your head. The bullets that snap close by your ears are the real killers. A few, losing power and slowing down, made a low buzzing sound.

Strange though it may seem, I wasn't scared or angry. I was beyond that. I didn't think I was going to die; I knew I was dead. There wasn't anything I could do about it. I wasn't a thinking human being. I had gone somewhere else. I wasn't firing the machine gun; *I was the machine gun*. Rod wasn't driving the truck; *Rod was the truck*.

I had melded with my weapon. I was no more human than the five-foot machine gun I was embracing. We were locked together, metal and flesh. Without that .50-cal, I would have quivered like the Askars, helpless in the storm. But with that weapon, I felt transported. I had something to do until the blackness came.

A .50-cal holds true out to half a mile. There was no wind and little need to fire high to arc the rounds onto targets. The gun shot rounds as big as cigars, and every fourth one was a glowing red tracer. Firing four- to eight-round bursts, I had walked rounds onto targets dozens of times up at Monti. The hills around Ganjigal were no different. I figured out roughly where a target was and let the .50-cal do the walking.

I wasn't paying any attention to the Afghan soldiers. Rod and I planned to keep driving east until we were obliterated or we found my team. Suddenly, with no warning, five or six Askars who were lying in a terrace about a hundred meters away leapt up and raced toward our truck. *Wham*, one was shot in the back and pitched for-

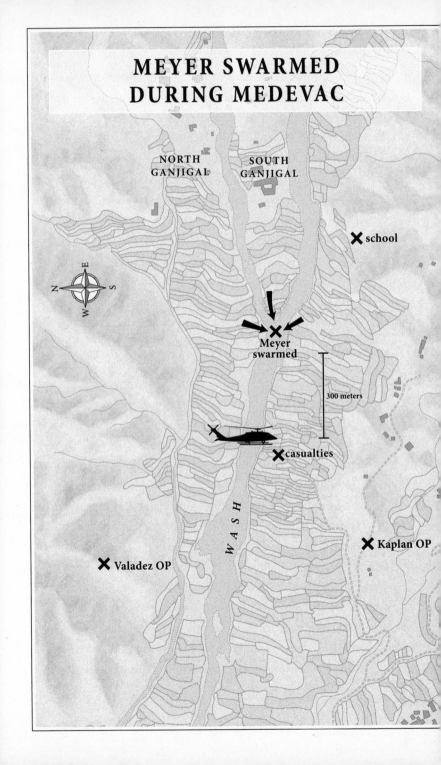

MEYER SWARMED DURING MEDEVAC

NORTH GANJIGAL

SOUTH GANJIGAL

✕ school

N E S W

Meyer swarmed

300 meters

✕ casualties

W A S H

✕ Valadez OP

✕ Kaplan OP

ward. *Wham,* a second man went down screaming. *Wham,* a third—then the fourth and the fifth.

I had never seen anything like it. Five men taken down in five seconds. There was so much screeching and shooting that I couldn't pick out the location of the weapon that shot them. To deliver such lethal grazing fire, the machine-gunner must have been hidden only a few hundred meters away, with a clear line of sight and his bipod firmly anchored. Yet whoever shot those men didn't raise his gun sights and stitch me. I knew he was looking at me, but I couldn't see him. There was nothing I could do. He let me live. Not one of his rounds even struck our truck. I can't explain it.

We couldn't see around the corners of the boomerang terrace walls, but Valadez, way up there, could see for us.

"They're coming at you!" he yelled over the radio. "I can see them closing from both sides. They're swarming you!"

In front of our truck, I saw a few guys sprinting across the wash from left to right, heads low. I don't think they saw us coming up behind them, or heard the truck engine over the din of the gunfire. They scurried too quickly for me to get off a burst. Glancing to my right, I looked smack into the eyes of five or six men in dirty man-dresses, crouched alongside a drainage ditch, not ten meters away. When I gaped at them, they ducked down like they were playing hide-and-seek.

It took me a few seconds to realize they were spreading out to seal off the open end of the horseshoe valley, ziplocking the frozen Askars inside a fire sack. Rod and I had blundered into their rear.

We were bouncing over rocks no faster than a man can run when a bearded dushman clutching an AK leapt out of a ditch and sprinted after us, like a man trying to catch a bus. My gun almost wouldn't swivel low enough to shoot him—the barrel was tilted down as far as it could go. I fired into his chest and he went down like he had hit a glass wall. A bullet doesn't blow a man back like in the movies. Either he stumbles on or he falls dead. This man fell dead.

Rod was yelling at me—maybe I was hypnotized for a second by the death. There was a guy trying to open the right door. I couldn't depress the .50-cal that low.

"I can't get him!" I yelled. "The gun won't go down enough!"

It takes the brain twelve thousandths of a second to react to danger. My mind was a complete blank. I had fired so many thousands of rounds that I didn't think what I was doing. Once you've practiced a motion long enough, it becomes second nature. Some researchers call it "expertise-induced amnesia." Athletes call it "being in the zone." I call it self-preservation. I grabbed my M4, leaned out, and shot the guy four or five times in the shoulder and the neck. It was like shooting a zombie. There was no shock power in the little 5.56-millimeter bullets. He fell to the ground.

I pivoted back to the .50-cal and grabbed the spade handle. The weapon, my hands, and my eyes were working as a trained unit, independent of my brain. *Man, sight picture, shoot.* You don't really look at the target. The enemy remains out of focus; you concentrate on the sight picture. *Man, sight picture, shoot.* I hit one or two guys next to the truck and the others ducked back into the ditch.

Valadez came back on the radio.

"Rod, watch your front!"

Rod was focused on keeping traction in the loose gravel. If the truck got stuck, even for a moment, we'd be toast. He looked ahead to see a bearded, hatless man in his mid-thirties, dressed in brick-red man-jams with a green chest rig full of ammo, running toward the truck and firing an AK at us from his hip.

"Hold on, Homey!" Rod yelled.

He hit the accelerator. The truck hit the man squarely in his chest. There was a bump, and then another bump under the tires.

"Holy shit!" Rod yelled. "I just ran over a guy."

"Back up and do it again!"

Ducking our firepower, the dushmen were pulling back into the terraces, jumping behind the walls, turkey-necking out to shoot at our blind spots. All had beards and none looked young. Most wore dirty clothes—some with Afghan Army trousers showing underneath. Many wore green chest rigs for ammunition and Afghan Army helmets. I would have shot more of them if I didn't have to look twice to make sure they weren't our guys.

A few hundred meters behind us, a monster-big Blackhawk was setting down in a terrace. I could see the blades turning and supposed it was a medevac. If the dushmen had the brains to ignore Rod and me and fire in the other direction, it would be a mess. The chopper was an easy mark for an RPG. I sprayed in a wide arc around the terraces to my right. I wasn't aiming; I just wanted the assholes to keep their heads down and their jihad thoughts on us. That chopper took off almost as soon as it landed—a great evac job by ballsy pilots.

The Askars remained frozen in the wash. We were all going to die if they stayed where they were and didn't fight back. We could maybe hold open the neck in the bottle for them to escape—if they would fight for it. Valadez kept shouting warnings to us, as I concentrated on shooting to my right and to the front. For every fifty rounds I was pumping out, we'd get two hundred back, including RPG rounds. One exploded about fifteen meters to our right front. Somehow the shrapnel didn't shred our front tire. I scanned the hills and the houses for the dust raised by the back blasts of the RPG tube—no luck. Some 107 rockets were mixed in, or maybe a recoilless rifle.

Rod was jerking the truck around to avoid their fire, but they couldn't miss us forever. I knew it wouldn't be a bullet; a red-hot chunk of jagged shrapnel would rip off my face, leaving it up to Rod to get out alone.

My sweaty right hand kept slipping off the gun's handgrip and butterfly trigger. When I wiped the sweat away, I realized it was red. I ducked down in the turret, letting my right arm dangle, to grab a bandage.

Rod looked at me in a startled way.

"You okay, man? You hit?"

"Yeah, yeah, I'm fine. Sweating like a pig is all. Go. Go."

I had been shot above the elbow—a bleeder that did no damage. The bone was fine. In a fight, adrenaline deadens the pain. I did a little wrapping and got back to shooting.

I had no idea where to go. My team was up ahead somewhere and out of radio contact. Each *whoosh* of an incoming RPG still caused me to involuntarily flinch. The air was sizzling and I had to scream for Rod to hear me.

"Do you see the team?"

"Negative!"

It was after eight in the morning and I was out of ideas. Then two small OH-58 Kiowa helicopters skimmed around my turret. The two-person Kiowa is about the size of an Austin Mini. It carries about two hundred rounds of .50-cal and a few small rockets. Think of an airborne motorcycle or an angry wasp.

The frustrated Kiowa pilots had been listening on their radios for the last forty minutes while Joyce dithered. Now that they'd been turned loose, the pilots couldn't do enough to help us. They'd provided the cover for Swenson's Command Group to get out of the wash, and now they were hovering above me. With my handheld, I made contact.

"This is Fox 3–3. I can't find my team. Four Marines are missing up in that village. I don't have a grid or radio contact with them."

"Three–3, this is Pale Horse," the pilot said. "Roger. We'll stay with you. Give us a vector."

"Pale Horse, the heaviest fire is coming from that white schoolhouse, grid 972 678."

"Three–3, we got it. Be right back."

The two Kiowas peeled off to the southeast and poured their remaining rockets into the schoolhouse. They then darted forward and buzzed back and forth over South Ganjigal. Dark smudges of smoke burst around them—the dushmen were using their RPGs as antiaircraft weapons.

I was swiveling the gun around, firing short bursts. When I saw a turkey-necker, I'd keep shooting until he went down or I had pulverized the terrace wall where he was hiding. I didn't have to aim down the gun sight; all I had to do was walk in the red tracers. The timing on the overheated gun was slipping, so I placed the bolt release in the up position and fired single shots.

The more fucked up things got, the more Rod and I started laughing. He was steering away from RPGs streaming at us and laughing, and I was shooting the big gun and laughing. Definitely crazy, but your emotions have to go somewhere.

The Kiowas, dipping low for their gun runs, looked too flimsy to last another minute. I'd hear a quick rattle of gunfire from them or toward them, and they'd peel off or zip straight up, bank sharply around, and zoom in again. The black puffs around them continued, but the enemy fire slackened on us as the Kiowas darted around. They were like a steel umbrella over us.

A few minutes later, Pale Horse came back on my net.

"Three–3, we're Winchester. We'll be back in fifteen mikes."

Winchester meant they had expended their munitions. They were too light to carry much, and they had been shooting at targets wherever they looked. The firing picked up. We were again the piñata. I climbed down from the turret to talk to Rod and Hafez. We had started in with six ammo cans. Now we were down to one. I had fired more than two thousand rounds.

"Guys, we need a new gun," I said. It was three steps forward, two back. As we turned around, I saw an Askar crawling feebly toward the road. We stopped and I hopped out. A PKM machine gun was tilling the ground around me, so I dodged back and forth until I reached him. One Kiowa, out of ammo, hovered above me and distracted the enemy, ignoring the RPG shells exploding in the air. I turned the Askar onto his back. Hit by three rounds in his upper chest and neck, he was gurgling and drowning in his own blood. I rolled him onto his side, and he died before I could pick him up.

Chapter 12

INTO THE WASH

I hopped back into the truck and we drove back down the wash to get ammo.

We had turned left out of the wash and onto the narrow track back to the casualty collection point.

The Afghans were turning back to their wounded. When I hopped out to help them, they asked if more helicopters were coming, or whether they should drive their casualties back to Joyce.

"I don't know," I said.

It wasn't that I didn't care, but I had my own problems. Where was my team? I looked around for Maj. Williams. He was sitting off to one side, wounded and in shock. There were four or five vehicles and at least twenty Askars milling around. These were our Afghans—we had come down from Monti together. I glanced hopefully from group to group. Hafez was asking if they had seen Lt. Johnson.

"They say the lieutenant is back in Ganjigal," Hafez said. "The team didn't make it out."

Shit!

Some of the wounded Askars had made it to the ORP where the U.S. Army platoon had stayed. They reported to the TOC that six Afghan soldiers were dead and nine wounded. That meant about thirty or forty were still pinned down in the valley or dead out there.

Hafez, Rod, and I drove back into the wash. Hafez could hand the ammo cans up to me—they're like big lunch boxes that clip to the gun. We were in good shape as long as the .50-cal didn't go out of whack again. We didn't have a kit for quickly changing the barrel, and the gauge for setting the gun's headspace wasn't in the toolbox.

A Ford Ranger driven by an Afghan policeman followed behind our Humvee. The Ranger would make do as an ambulance to ferry out the wounded. As we entered the wash, we passed Swenson and Fabayo in another Ranger truck, heading to the casualty point with two or three wounded or dead Afghans piled in the back. Swenson brought back two dead jihadists, too. That proves he's a nicer guy than I am.

Good for them, I thought; *those guys are doing something.*

Askars were walking out as we drove back in. Some were dazed, others limping, some leaning on each other. Many had tied a cloth around an arm or a leg. With their chests protected by body armor, they thought they weren't badly hit. But they were inviting death within an hour or two. A bullet wound in the arm or leg often doesn't bleed profusely. Instead your blood drips out steadily, your blood pressure drops, your body goes into shock, and you die. Doc Layton had given them classes for a month, but in the chaos of combat, they had forgotten everything.

I wanted to ignore the Askars, because somewhere, farther up the wash, my team was fighting to stay alive. I'd promised to get them, and Rod and I had the only gun truck willing and able to go in. I wanted to pretend I didn't see the bleeding. Besides, they were not far from the collection point, where they might get help or a ride out.

We'd gone only another hundred meters when I saw an Afghan soldier huddled behind a rock. No other Askar was around. We were the advisors, which comes with a responsibility, like being parents.

I had no choice.

"Hold up, Rod."

I climbed down from the turret and ran over to the Askar. He'd taken a bullet in the thigh and was slowly bleeding out. I kept a stack of tourniquets in my medpack and knew how to apply them. I wrapped a tourniquet around his thigh. In my frustration, I twisted it extra tight and he screamed.

"Hafez, tell him to shut up," I said. "Hurting is better than dying."

Not the most soothing bedside manner. I knew I was being unfair. If someone cinched a thin strap around my leg and twisted as hard as he could, I'd scream, too.

If you're a grunt, you will come face to face with horrendous gore. You have to steel yourself to seeing mangled bodies and smelling blood. Doctors and nurses cope with screaming and suffering every day. I had dressed out dozens of deer. You learn to dissociate from the task when you're pulling out warm guts or cutting off slabs of dripping meat, with the blood sticking to your hands.

Doc Layton had kidded me for being a hospital pack rat. He was the corpsman, but my medpack, stuffed with everything I could scrounge, was bigger than his. I had taken the Combat Lifesaver course while stationed with my battalion. Plus, on a sniper team, you don't have a corpsman, so I had to learn a variety of emergency skills. It was interesting, so I tried to learn as much as I could, especially about trauma.

Hafez and I moved the moaning Askar into the back of the Ranger behind us, and we both drove back to the casualty collection point. It was now about nine in the morning and Swenson and Fabayo had come forward again in their Ford Ranger.

The Kiowas had rearmed and come back on station, directing us toward another wounded. Like it or not, we had been pressed into the ambulance business. The Kiowa commanded by Chief Warrant Officer Yossarian Silano—a good name for a guy in a crazy war—had been a Marine grunt before becoming an Army pilot. His bird was easy to talk to and directed me where to go, sometimes hovering so low I could just about reach up and touch his skids. He was covering my rear whenever I got out of the truck.

Twice, Hafez and I got out, climbed up the sides of terraces, found the Askars, and lugged them down the terrace walls to the wash. After we'd loaded two into a Ranger, my brain finally kicked in: I couldn't be the gunner and the corpsman at the same time. I didn't need Hafez out there in the fields with me. Rod, though, needed someone on the gun.

"Hafez, will you take over the .50-cal?" I said. "I can do more good on the ground."

Hafez climbed into the turret. I dragged an Askar to the road, and Hafez waved to an Afghan truck to pick him up. But the .50-cal was acting up and Hafez had difficulty clearing the jams. He was jacking the bolt back and I was nervous that he'd pull off the back plate with the bolt locked to the rear. If he did, the pressure of his next and last burst would drive the plate into his chest. To coax the gun back into firing shape, every so often I'd slip and slide up into the turret—blood from my arm and the wounded Askars had spattered everywhere inside the truck—and try to reset the gun.

The incoming fire didn't stop. The machine-gunners were aiming at movement. They were shooting short bursts, with good fire discipline. Some gunners seemed to have spotters hidden in the houses.

They weren't using tracers, so no green rounds gave away their positions. Without tracers, though, they couldn't adjust well. A machine-gunner shooting from five hundred meters away couldn't tell if he was missing me to the right or the left. Plus, firing at a downward angle of 30 degrees, they were overcompensating.

I knew by the sounds of the bullets when a gunner was zeroing in on me. When puffs of dirt spurted close, I'd find a depression and lie flat. Not seeing me, the gunner would grow bored. I'd wait until the dirt kicked up farther off before moving again.

With Swenson driving one truck and Rod the other, we shuttled around for maybe ten or fifteen minutes, a few Afghan trucks following and at least two Kiowas buzzing overhead. About six had been sent to help us. While two covered us, another pair waited on the other side of the ridge and the third pair rearmed at a nearby base. The pilots were fearless. Knowing my team was lost, they were running search patterns twenty feet off the ground so that they could identify each body.

Many of my Askars were lying prone, doing nothing, not returning fire. I'd trained them on the M16s, but they weren't comfortable with them. Some had ripped through all their magazines, while others didn't want to attract attention by shooting. I left the able-bodied to fend for themselves, because I couldn't organize them without getting Hafez out of the truck to interpret.

To the enemy gunners up in the hills above us, our trucks probably looked a little like beetles scurrying around, swerving from one terrace to the next. Maybe they thought it was like a video game as they tried to hit us. They were doing their best, and they were experienced shooters who had crossed over from Pakistan for this event.

. . .

Swenson and Fabayo stopped their Ford Ranger next to us to talk over our next move. Behind us, an Afghan truck was shuttling wounded back to the collection point.

"Lieutenant," I said to Fabayo. "Can you replace Hafez on the .50-cal? That'll free him up to talk to the Afghans, and I got a sighting on another wounded."

Fabayo got into our turret and Hafez got on the radio. I hopped in with Swenson. He was driving with a handset jammed to his ear, yelling back and forth to the Kiowas. The Ranger had taken a beating. The shocks were absolutely gone. Rounds had gone through the suspension, door, door handle, rear window, and cab. I pointed to a terrace about a hundred meters off to our left front.

"Stop!" I said. "I think that's where I saw the guy. I'll go look."

Swenson had torn the ligament in his right knee and his shins were peppered with shrapnel, so he stayed behind the wheel and I hopped out.

"Don't go far," Swenson said.

I climbed up a terrace wall and followed the contours of the field around a corner to a body lying facedown. On the man's hands were green gloves with the fingers cut out. I knew even before I rolled him over that it was Dodd Ali, my closest Afghan friend. He was due to take leave in a few weeks. He had left on bad terms with his mother, who was sure he would be killed. Finally, after two years, she had relented and invited him back to the farm for a visit.

He'd been hit in the face. When I looked at his dull eyes, I lost my concentration and I knelt there for a moment, oblivious. He was a little guy, too small for his body armor. He and I had rigged up two tourniquets to hold the armor close around his chest. I knelt down to untie the tourniquets. I needed them for other guys, and I needed to get the heavy armor off him so I could carry him to the truck.

DODD ALI FOUND

NORTH GANJIGAL

SOUTH GANJIGAL

WASH

✖ Dodd Ali

I felt a tap as something hit my left shoulder. It didn't register at first. It was like I had been hit with a light stone. I glanced up to see a tough-looking Afghan with a long black beard glaring down at me. He was wearing a dirty gray man-dress, a flak jacket, and an Afghan Army helmet. He was pointing an AK at my head, gesturing for me to stand up. In broken English, he was telling me to drop my rifle.

"Come," he said, waving the barrel of his AK in my face.

I couldn't believe that I'd screwed up so badly. All I could think of was that my head would be sawed off and held up on TV.

No way. I'd die right where I was, right now. I had been dead for a few hours anyway. The borrowed time was up, that's all.

My rifle was resting on my left thigh, pointing in his direction. The stubby grenade launcher was attached to the underside of the barrel.

I raised one arm like I was going to surrender and pulled the trigger of the launcher with my free thumb. The 40-millimeter grenade shot forward the two feet to his armored vest. It didn't explode. Instead it knocked him back. Stunned and with the breath slammed out of him, he staggered back and fell on his side. For a few seconds, I thought the blow had killed him. No such luck.

As I pushed myself erect, he drew in a big breath and stirred. I kicked at his face, losing my balance and falling on top of him. We were both on the ground, wrestling. Afghan tribesmen have legs like steel from climbing mountains all day, all their lives, so I had to keep his legs off me. I pinned his elbows and blocked his reach for his AK. I was pushing my helmeted head into his chest so he couldn't gouge my eyes. At any second, I figured, that grenade would explode and the both of us could stop worrying about any of this.

I pawed the ground with my right hand and found a rock the size of a baseball. I clutched it and swung blindly at his face. The blow stunned him. Before he could recover, I pushed off his chest, lifted the rock high in my right fist, and smashed it down like a hammer, breaking his front teeth. He looked me in the eyes, the fight knocked out of him, his head not moving. We both knew it was over. I drew back my arm and drove the stone down, crushing his left cheekbone. He went limp. I pushed up on my knees and hit him with more force. The blow caved in the left side of his forehead. I smashed his face again and again, driven by pure primal rage.

I turned back to Dodd Ali. I tried to pick up my friend, but he was stiff and I couldn't get a firm grip. I fumbled with the tourniquets and when I couldn't untie them, I cut them loose, pulled off the armor, and trudged back toward the truck, dragging Dodd Ali behind me.

When I came around the corner of the terrace, I was back into the fire. Once again I heard the bursts of PKM rounds cracking past. They sounded high, so I paid them no mind and continued pulling Dodd Ali. I was in a semi-trance, emotionally and physically drained. I shut out the world and concentrated on tugging the body. I'd bend over, get a good grip, and haul backward for a few meters. I'd then stand erect and stretch out my cramped muscles before bending over again. I'd got it into my mind that all I had to do was get Dodd Ali to the truck. That was the goal line. *Finish the game.*

I had developed a rhythm to my tugs, so it took a while before I realized that Swenson was yelling at me. I'd forgotten he had been sitting out there, the only target on the battlefield, shifting the truck back and forth, waiting for me.

"We gotta move, man!" he yelled. "Let's get out of here."

I was trying to pull Dodd Ali into the back of the Ranger, but I didn't have the strength. I was beat. I leaned against the pickup.

Swenson hopped out, picked up Dodd Ali, and rolled his stiff body into the open back. He pushed me into the passenger seat and slid back behind the wheel. He paused for a second, looking at my sagging, sweat-running face.

The Ford Ranger was a shiny tin can bobbing in the middle of the wash, with machine-gun crews competing to perforate us. It was a hot day and the windows were rolled down. I know this sounds ridiculous, but it sounded like one or two bullets zipped through the cab and missed us both. Then Swenson laughed a maniac's cackle, and I joined in. *We are fucking nuts!*

The pickup was now definitely too banged up to continue. If we broke an axle or lost cooling fluid, we'd be quickly finished off. We jounced down the wash and turned left into the shelter of the rough trace.

Kunar River (Monti at center left). *(Capt. Jacob Kerr)*

Combat Outpost Monti (Afghan section at lower left). *(Capt. Jacob Kerr)*

Big Mike Meyer, Dakota Meyer, and Bing West at Big Mike's farm. *(Bing West)*

Dakota Meyer,
October 2009.
(Bing West)

Dakota behind the .50-cal in the turret of a Humvee. *(Bing West)*

Dodd Ali and Dakota.
(Dakota Meyer)

Dab Khar Valley. *(Capt. Jacob Kerr)*

The kill zone at Dab Khar
Valley. *(Capt. Jacob Kerr)*

Lt. Mike Johnson. *(Dakota Meyer)*

Doc Layton.
(Dakota Meyer)

Dakota and Staff Sgt. Kenefick.
(Dakota Meyer)

Team Monti. *(Dakota Meyer)*

A typical village elder.
(Capt. William Swenson)

The mountains at Dab Khar. *(Dakota Meyer)*

The fatal wash at Ganjigal. *(Capt. William Swenson)*

The slopes of Ganjigal.
(Capt. William Swenson)

Capt. William Swenson.
(Capt. William Swenson)

Dakota and President Obama at the Medal of Honor ceremony.
(AP Photo/Pablo Martinez Monsivais)

Dab Khar fighters: Gunnery Sgt. Kevin Devine, Lt. Jake Kerr, Cpl. Dakota Meyer, Staff Sgt. Richards, Sgt. 1st Class Dennis Jeffords. *(Capt. Jacob Kerr)*

Dakota and a young admirer.
(Dakota Meyer)

Dakota walking back from the Freedom Tower, September 2011.
(Marine Sgt. Randall Clinton)

"For those who gave all.
Semper Fi."
*(Marine Sgt. Randall
Clinton)*

The memorial at Monti.
(Dakota Meyer)

Chapter 13

PRIMAL

When we reached the casualty collection point, the Askars rushed over to take the body and Swenson got out to talk to the Army platoon leader. A second Blackhawk had landed and taken out a half-dozen of the most seriously wounded Askars. At 0930—three hours after Team Monti was cut off from the Command Group in the wash—the TOC at Joyce finally reported up the chain of command that four Americans were missing. The Afghan battalion had sent in a small quick-reaction force from Joyce. I looked around, but I didn't see any American commanders or soldiers sent up from Joyce.

I walked over to Maj. Williams and 1st Sgt. Garza, who were sitting off to one side, to be briefed on their plan. It was time for the advisors to take charge and bring out my team.

When I was only a few feet away from him, Garza started yelling loudly.

"We gotta get back in there. I'm ready to go!"

I looked closely at him. His eyes were unfocused and his sentences came in short rushes. His face was bruised and, although I didn't see blood trickling out of his ears, I knew he was concussed.

"You better take it easy, First Sergeant," I said. "You're not in good shape."

"Get out of my way. I'm going back in."

He wasn't making sense. He couldn't fight effectively.

"No, First Sergeant, you're not going back in."

"Yes, I am!"

"No, you're getting medevaced out."

"Who's going to stop me? You can't make me."

Maj. Williams stepped in.

"I can make you, First Sergeant," he said. "You're not going back into the fight."

I stopped an Afghan truck and told the driver to take Garza back to Camp Joyce. The civilian reporter came up to tell me he'd stay to help.

"No, you're not staying," I said, thinking the last thing I needed was to get guys killed searching for a reporter if he got lost or separated again.

"You're not staying," Williams said to the reporter.

Garza and the reporter were leaving. That left Maj. Williams. He was sitting down, with his arms wrapped around his drawn-up knees. I looked at the inside of his left forearm. The bleeding had stopped. I waited for him to give orders to organize the search for my team.

"We lost today, Corporal," he said, rocking back and forth. "We lost today."

We lost today? I thought to myself. *I don't know about you, but my day isn't over yet.*

Maj. Williams climbed into the truck and left the battlefield.

I was the only American left at the casualty collection point. Fabayo, Rod, and Swenson had gone back to get a new truck and reinforcements. Hafez had gone with them. Without him to translate, I couldn't organize the Afghans.

I still had my M4 with the grenade launcher and plenty of ammo. The battery in my handheld radio was holding strong and I had good communications with the Kiowas. I had wasted enough time. I headed back into the fight. It was only half a mile from the casualty collection point to South Ganjigal. The enemy machine-gunners would be looking for the next Humvee to enter the wash. If I cut due east across the terraces, they might not see me, or they might ignore me. I just wasn't staying here.

As I walked down the track, Silano's Kiowa swooped down and hovered over my head.

"Fox 3–3, this is Pale Horse, what are you doing?"

"Pale Horse, I'm going to Ganjigal," I said. "Can you scout ahead?"

"Fox 3–3, that is not a good idea. Hold where you are. Highlander is on the move to your pos. I will direct him. I repeat, you hold where you are."

Highlander was the radio call sign for Captain Swenson. He was trying to gather reinforcements. He had pulled aside the lieutenant in charge of the quick-reaction platoon.

"Mount up," Swenson had told him. "You're no help back here. We need your firepower."

"I can't," the lieutenant said. "The TOC says we're to cover the vehicles."

Swenson grabbed the lieutenant's 50-watt radio to call Joyce. The TOC told the platoon to move into the valley. Swenson, Fabayo, Rod, and Hafez then hopped into an undamaged Humvee to drive back in, but the platoon did not follow. Instead, the platoon leader again called back to Joyce and somehow received permission to remain in the rear, out of the fight.

It was about ten in the morning when Rod drove the Humvee up to where I was waiting. Fabayo was in the turret and Swenson was in the front command seat, working two radios, one to the Kiowas and the other to Shadow on the southern ridge. I climbed into the rear next to Hafez, who was talking in Pashto on his handheld. We started up the wash, with two or three Afghan trucks a few hundred meters behind us.

There was a pall of smoke in the truck from the never-ending machine-gun fire up the turret. All of us were gritty and bloody, but we had plenty of bottles of water in the truck. Swenson was directing the Kiowas in a terrace-by-terrace search. Whenever the pilots saw wounded Askars, they'd radio, "Spot!" Rod would drive in front of them to act as a shield. Fabayo was shooting. The main gun wasn't working, so he was using the lighter 240 machine gun.

There were still so many wounded to grab that we were again losing our focus on the lost team, but you can't let people bleed to death in front of you. I'd jump out to administer aid and pull the wounded out of the line of fire behind our truck. The Askars tended to cluster in groups of two to four, spread out along the terrace walls. As I moved around to different groups of men hunkered down, I'd look for spent cartridges at their feet. If I didn't see the yellow glint of spent brass, I'd urge them to shoot. There's easy body language for that.

On a battlefield, you have to be careful for IEDs where you walk. Luckily, unlike down in the south, the dushmen in the mountains didn't sow mines in the fields, probably because Askars and Americans rarely patrolled out in the middle of nowhere.

I didn't know whether an Askar lying in a terrace was wounded or dead. I came across two in rigor mortis, and I dragged them by their armpits down to the wash to be picked up. I tried not to look at their faces. The sight of one soldier with both legs blown off got to me for a minute. I wondered what weapon could have done that. There was already that cloying stink to a few of the corpses and those black flies with the green heads—flying slugs—were sucking up the blood and rotting flesh. I don't know where those flies of death come from, but I wish I could poison or burn them all.

With the wounded, I tried to stop the bleeding. That was all I took time to do. I didn't strip off their gear or check them for concussion. I just looked for where the blood was squirting out and tried to stop it. I'd started the day with fourteen or sixteen tourniquets, and I used them all. I put four on one guy who had lost his left arm and his left leg below the knee. He survived.

As I mentioned, it was Ramadan. Even when they were wounded and dehydrated, about one out of three Askars wouldn't drink. Hafez would call forward an Afghan truck for the evacuation, while Fabayo provided suppressive fire. Hafez thought we pulled out about ten or twelve wounded. One Askar, shot in the neck, sounded like he was slurping through a straw. There was nothing I could do except listen to him strangle to death.

I picked up four or five dead from the gang I'd kidded around with at Monti. I tried to place the wounded on top of the dead in the Afghan trucks, but sometimes I didn't have time to do it properly—the PKM fire persisted. I was amazed how much ammo the enemy had stored in the hills.

At one point, two F-15s roared low through the valley, opening their afterburners to create a hell of a lion's roar. The pilots wouldn't drop any bombs. They were concerned we didn't know where my missing team was, and didn't agree with Swenson's request that they drop their ordnance near the machine guns up on the ridgelines. 'Bye.

An air controller with the Army scout-sniper team, Shadow 4, on the south ridge kept two to four Kiowas with Hellfire missiles hovering on standby waiting their turn to enter the valley. Shadow, angry that fire missions kept getting denied, also fended off the endless questions from the TOC at Joyce.

At one point, I heard Swenson let out a sarcastic laugh.

"Shadow 4, ask the TOC," he radioed, "what will they fucking give me?"

By 1030, the enemy fire from the ridges had slackened considerably. The pilots knew my team wasn't located in any hillside cave, so they concentrated their rocket and gun runs on the higher elevations. An Apache helicopter, with greater firepower than a Kiowa, came on station for a while. Fabayo tried to direct it, but lacking a GPS, he could only radio that the enemy were "everywhere." The Apache ran low on fuel before it could acquire targets.

The pilots wouldn't shoot blindly, though, at the terraces and compounds on the valley floor. When they saw a wounded Askar out in the terraces, they would say "Spot" over the radio as they flew over the body to guide us to the spot.

Inside the villages, the Army pilots ran astonishing risks to find my team. A Kiowa would swoop down toward the compounds, flare back at rooftop level, and putter down the alleyways at twenty miles an hour, allowing the pilots to peer into every backyard and into every window. Bearded and unarmed dushmen, close enough to see the sweat on their faces, glared back through the windows. After a Kiowa crept past, the dushmen shot at it from the rear. Not knowing which house my team was in, the pilots didn't return fire. There weren't any civilians wandering around. That day, the people of Gan-jigal reverted to the traditional Pashtun way—they were fighting the outsiders. Five hours into the battle, no one was out for a stroll to check on the growth of the wheat.

As the day grew hotter, we gradually cleared the valley of casualties. Over thirty wounded or dead were evacuated. Driving around, we encountered less fire. When we finally pulled within a few hundred meters of the Ganjigal hamlets, I saw small knots of Askars from Monti tucked into defensive positions. They had conserved their ammunition, held their ground, and five hours into the battle, continued to skirmish with the dushmen. Great fire discipline.

My team had to be nearby. The Kiowas were bobbing up and down, skittering out of the way of small-arms bursts from windows.

I saw something blinking and glinting among the houses midway up the northern slope.

"A signal mirror!" I said. "We've found them!"

"We have a signal," Swenson radioed to the pilots. "At our ten o'clock, the sixth, no, the seventh terrace up. The window to the left of the large rusty compound door."

Like a darting hawk, a Kiowa flared upward, peeled to the left, and swooped down, hovering alongside the compound.

"Negative," the pilot said. "It's a shiny cooking pot hanging on a clothesline."

A few minutes later, Staff Sgt. Valadez, in the north observation perch, spotted an orange panel on the roof of a compound on the south side of the wash.

Pale Horse darted over in his Kiowa.

"Negative," Silano radioed to us. "It's an ice cooler."

Rod eased the truck up to the top of a crest to get a better look around. We were worn down and testy with each other. The day had gone on for a few months. In the turret, Fabayo was firing in two-round bursts.

"Vary the rate," I snapped at him. We didn't need another jammed gun.

"Shut up!" he yelled, kicking at my head. "I'm a lieutenant and you're a corporal. Don't tell me what to do."

"I'm telling you," I said, "the gun will jam if you keep that up. What will your dumb ass do then?"

It was no more personal than one lineman yelling at another in the heat of a football game.

Where are they? Where is my team?

"Why are we sitting here, doing nothing?" I yelled at Swenson.

"We're waiting for reinforcements," Swenson said.

"That's bullshit!" I said. "The Army's not coming. They haven't come all day and you know it."

We had reached our snapping points, physically worn down and mentally fatigued from constantly reading the maps, figuring out and calling ten-digit grid coordinates to one set of pilots after another, trying to come up with a search pattern for combing a hundred terraces. Emotionally, we were tapped out—a captain, a lieutenant, and a corporal squabbling, with no idea where our four lost brothers were and furious that we were out there on our own, treated over the radio from the TOC at Joyce as if we were a nuisance.

With two Kiowas constantly buzzing overhead, the enemy fire had decreased. I thought it was time to move into the damn village. Swenson was silent for a moment.

"All right," he said, "we'll move up. You sit tight."

We hadn't gone far when we saw another wounded Afghan off to our left. I got out to get him when a PKM dialed in on me. Seeing that I was pinned down, Pale Horse came to my rescue, making repeated strafing runs until the enemy fire stopped. I got the wounded man into an Afghan truck and ran back to our truck.

The TOC had known for hours that my team was missing. That key information had finally trickled up the chain of command. How could it not, since every helicopter entering the valley was searching for the team? Eventually the word reached a three-star general hundreds of miles away. This prompted a declaration of "personal recovery" or DUSTWUN (duty status whereabouts unknown). The Special Operations Command responded immediately by dispatching Apache attack helicopters and Air Force helicopters with pararescue jumpers, or PJs—an elite force of tough commandos.

Chapter 14

TEAM MONTI

By eleven in the morning, helicopters were swooping in low from different directions. A big Blackhawk was hovering low to the ground to our right front. The pilots thought they had located my team and were trying to land an Air Force para-rescue team. After an orange smoke grenade was pitched out to mark the spot, PKM fire narrowly missed the chopper. To avoid being shot down, it swung away without landing anyone. The pilot tried from another angle with the same result.

"Highlander, this is Pale Horse. That smoke is attracting too much incoming. I'll mark the spot by hovering above it."

Our Humvee was idling in the wash. Fabayo was firing at the south ridge, where a PKM was still shooting at some Askars. There were only a dozen compounds on the knob of South Ganjigal off to our right, with small terraces spread out like a fan in front of the compounds.

Maybe, I thought, the team retreated back into the houses. "I'm going to search those compounds," I said.

"Stay buttoned up," Swenson said.

"They're my team," I said, "and I'm going to find them, not sit here wasting time."

"I'm an Army captain, Corporal," Swenson said. "I'm giving you a direct order. Stay in the damn truck. We're all here to find them. It's not just you."

The rebuke stung, because I knew he was right. Climbing up the terraces and busting down compound doors—with no one watching my back—I wouldn't have lasted long. I sat where I was and fumed. Steam was coming out of my helmet.

I was pissed at this long-haired captain, the way I'd sometimes get with a coach. I didn't like what he was saying, but I didn't disagree with his right to say it. I didn't know what step I could take next. Swenson was the outsider. He lived in a different camp. He didn't even know our names, where we were from, or what military skills we did or didn't have. He was our leader, and yet he didn't know us. We hadn't even been introduced. I didn't know how to get through to him.

I did know he had gotten the Command Group out and plunged right back into the fire. We were in this together, sitting there in a tense, silent standoff. We watched as Silano, the lead pilot, brought his Kiowa down to a few feet above a trench and hovered there.

"Highlander, we've spotted five bodies . . ."

I'd heard all I needed. I jumped out the door and sprinted across the field to the right, opening some distance before Swenson yelled at me. I ignored him, knowing he'd be right behind me. A PKM shifted to me when I was halfway across the terrace. I hopped over a terrace wall and fell into a deep, well-constructed trench.

I landed next to Gunny Johnson, and my heart stopped. He was lying on his back with his arms outspread, his eyes open but never to see anything again on this earth.

A few feet farther on, I came across the body of an Afghan interpreter who had traveled with our team. I felt sick to my stomach. I knew what I would see next.

Lt. Johnson lay on his back, with his eyes closed. He looked peaceful, despite the entry wounds in his right shoulder. Doc Layton lay on top of him, with medical supplies scattered around. I rolled him over. Doc had taken a three-round burst in the right cheek.

Off to the right, Staff Sgt. Kenefick was lying facedown, his GPS with a busted screen clutched in his left hand. His mouth was open and full of dirt. I think he was yelling out his grid location—the numbers I heard over the radio four hours earlier—when he was shot in the back of his head.

The team was wiped out. Their bodies were stiff and cold. Most of their gear was gone—weapons, helmets, radios. The 240 machine gun was missing, but Lt. Johnson's pack was full of linked ammo. No one had fired the gun I was supposed to be carrying.

I had never believed it would end like this. My mind refused to accept what I was seeing. Hour after hour, I had imagined them holed up inside a stone house, shielded from RPG blasts, exchanging gunfire with dushmen who knew better than to rush them.

Swenson was standing above the trench. We were taking random incoming and he was watching for movement among the houses. He talked into his radio for a few seconds, then bent down and picked up some of the team's gear. He didn't say a word. He left me alone with them.

I hoisted the staff sergeant over my right shoulder. He was heavy and I fell once. He landed on top of me. I got up and carried him to an Afghan truck, carefully tucking him into the open bed. I stood there for a minute, suddenly beat. As I turned away from the truck, Hafez put his hand on my shoulder.

"The Askars say you carried out their dead. Now, they want to help you."

Five or six of us returned to the trench, while the damn PKM kept shooting at us. I carried Gunny Johnson back; the Askars took Lt. Johnson and Doc Layton. Swenson lugged back the rest of the equipment.

After six hours, it was over, and I felt as empty as a balloon without air. Hafez took me aside.

"They have gone to a better place," he said. "Don't cry. The Askars will take it as weakness."

No way I was going to cry. But at that moment, I didn't feel like killing anyone, either. I wasn't angry or bitter, just deflated and exhausted, as though I had run a marathon and couldn't remember why I wanted to do it. I was too damned tired to stand.

Still taking fire, we left the valley in a convoy of about four trucks. Rod stopped near the casualty collection point, where we talked with Capt. Kaplan and Cpl. Norman, who had walked down from their observation post. Staff Sgts. Valadez and Miller radioed that they were coming down from their perch, too. Everyone was accounted for. We had shuttled in and out of the valley five, six, or seven times that morning, depending on which of us you asked. It was all a fog. No senior American officer or pursuit force had come forward from Joyce. Capt. Swenson said he would stay to wrap things up.

Hafez and I climbed into the back of an Afghan truck carrying my dead brothers. I held Staff Sgt. Kenefick with my left hand, and Lt. Johnson rested on my right arm. As we bounced down the track, we passed villagers returning to Ganjigal. Some started to laugh, pointing at my dead friends. I reached for my rifle.

"Don't," Hafez said, holding my arm. "Not worth it."

. . .

When we arrived back at Camp Joyce, I walked into the battalion aid station to get the body bags. Maj. Williams rushed up and clutched at my body armor.

"Tell me they're not all dead, not all of them."

"They're all dead," I said, removing his hand.

I walked outside, where my friend Sgt. Charles Bokis was waiting. Bokis said, "I'll give you a hand."

We walked back to the bodies. Sgt. Maj. Jimmy Carabello, the top enlisted man at Joyce, hastened up and put his hands firmly on my shoulders, trying to steer me away.

"You don't have to do this, Devil Dog. My guys will make sure it's done right."

That wasn't how to end it. If I had died, I'd want Lt. Johnson and Staff Sgt. Kenefick to put me in the bag.

"I'll finish it," I said.

Bokis and I carry the bodies into the back next to the freezers, take off their battle gear, and dig through their pockets, marking items for shipment to their families. I take a chevron from Staff Sgt. Kenefick and attach it to my dog tags. Funny, we had started out not liking each other a thousand years ago.

We clean them up as best we can, wiping the blood and dirt off their faces, taking off their field gear, straightening out their camouflage uniforms, and placing each in a black body bag. We mark the name at the head, drape an American flag over each bag, bow our heads in prayer, and drive them to the helo pad.

Chapter 15

DAB KHAR

After the helicopter had taken my brothers on their first leg home, an Army captain took me aside and asked how I was feeling. She was a psychologist who meant well, asking me to fly back to the main base at Bagram to "decompress." I expressed my thanks and turned away.

Sgt. Maj. Carabello, who had been watching me, took me over to his hooch and offered me his cell phone to call home. I didn't want to talk to my dad. What was I supposed to say? That my brothers were dead and I was alive? I shook my head no and started to leave.

"Devil Dog, wash off that blood," he said. "You'll feel better."

In a latrine mirror, I see a blood-streaked monster looking back at me. I'd shoot without a moment's hesitation if I saw that face outside the wire. My cammies look like rust and my red hands feel like sticky glue. The copper smell of blood hangs on me. I slosh hot water all over me. I make a mess of the floor.

In the battalion aid station, an American Army doctor had treated seven Afghan troops for bullet wounds, two for concussions, and two for RPG and rocket shrapnel. He had evacuated another nine with more serious wounds and set the two dead aside for burial. I walked a few hundred meters to the Afghan side of the camp, made my way to the makeshift morgue, and helped to tidy up two dead Askars.

After that, I drifted over to the Afghan mess hall, dumped some rice and carrots on a cardboard tray, and climbed up to the roof. Hafez came up, with several Askars behind him. We didn't say much as the sun went down.

When I arrived at Monti the next day, Lt. Kerr told me he had wanted to throw up when he heard how the TOC had stiffed us. All the soldiers at Monti felt the same way. They all offered to help pack up my guys' personal belongings.

"I appreciate it," I said, "but they're my brothers. I have to do it."

When I walked into the hooch, all the gear was scattered about, exactly as we had left it. Lt. Johnson's skimpy PT shorts that we all kidded him about were on his rack, Doc Layton's CDs on the table, and Staff Sgt. Kenefick's computer on his rack.

Maj. Williams had sent Bokis and Staff Sgt. Richards up to Monti with me. Together we sorted, marked, and stored the belongings of my brothers. After that, I walked outside, fidgeted around, and finally went into the ammo bunker to count up our munitions and keep myself busy. I heard a gunshot over at the burn pit and what sounded like my pup Annie yelp, then another gunshot.

There was an order to shoot all dogs on base, but the 1st sergeant in the ops center had assured me Annie would be fine. Still, after the shots, I walked outside and called for her.

A sergeant was rounding the corner with his shotgun slung.

"That wasn't my dog you shot, was it?" I asked.

"No, it wasn't yours," he replied, trying to get around me.

"Let's make sure," I said.

We walked around the corner, and I looked at her lying on top of the burning trash.

"You motherfucker," I said, "how about I lay your stupid ass down and shoot *you*? She was giving you kisses and wagging her tail while you carried her over here and shot her twice, wasn't she—you piece of shit!"

"First sergeant ordered me to do it," he said.

"He did what?" I said as I walked off.

I stormed down the hill, looking for the man. Gunny Kevin Devine, Kerr's platoon sergeant, saw me and fell in step beside me. He knew what had happened.

"Be cool, Devil Dog," he said. "Don't fuck up your life."

The 1st sergeant who had killed Annie was standing outside the ops center, smoking a cigar, with a stupid smirk on his dumbass face. As I headed for him, Gunny Devine, who had twenty pounds of muscle on me, grabbed my shoulder. He made it plain he was going to wrestle me to the ground. I settled for smacking the sandbag next to the 1st sergeant's face, and Devine pulled me away before I committed a court-martial offense.

It probably wasn't a good idea that I was bunking in the hooch. Bokis and Sgt. Richards were good company, but I didn't want them to think they had to babysit me. The first few days back, I avoided even trying to sleep. As long as I was awake and doing something, I thought I was okay.

Each night, Kerr and Devine led their platoon—a platoon of strong men—through hours of pain in the weight room, and they dragged me along. My muscles were burning and Kerr was yelling for one more lift and then another. The pain was a relief. It stopped my thinking.

After the others showered and turned in, I'd wander around the quiet base, visiting with the Askars in the sentry tower, improving my Pashto. A few new advisors moved into the hooch. I never got close to them. My bad. I was standoffish—didn't feel at ease with them. I didn't want any new friends.

As to Ganjigal: Some Special Forces teams entered the village in the late afternoon, many hours after the ambush. By then, the Taliban had collected their dead and wounded and hiked back into Pakistan.

Ganjigal was one of the deadliest small-arms battles of the Afghanistan war. We lost five advisors. In addition to Team Monti, Army Sgt. 1st Class Westbrook had died of his wounds. Eight Askars were killed and thirteen seriously wounded by rifle, machine-gun, and RPG fire. Enemy losses to small arms were probably of a similar number. There were no IEDs, no bombs, and very few artillery shells. Bullets caused most of the casualties. Ganjigal was a mountain fight from an earlier century.

The Taliban leader, Rahman, crowed over the Taliban radio about his great victory. But the American and Afghan commanders decided not to launch a retaliatory raid; they didn't want to draw attention to our defeat and to the lack of fire support. I thought their passive approach was wrong. If you were a villager anywhere in Kunar Province, what would you think after Ganjigal? We should have hit back at a Taliban camp.

The Askars decided they could not trust the Americans to support them. So they didn't want to patrol unless they were accompanied by U.S. Army soldiers, not just advisors. As for the Americans, Capt. Paco Bryant, the commander of Dog Company, didn't want to send his soldiers into a village like Ganjigal if they weren't going to hold it.

"As soon as you leave, it will be back in enemy hands within two or three days," he said, "and that's not worth a soldier's life."

The U.S. high command decided that any patrol into a capillary valley like Ganjigal required helicopter support, and a PowerPoint brief sent to battalion and brigade headquarters. As a result, the pace of patrolling by Askars and by Americans dropped dramatically.

Finally, I had another chance. Col. Daniel Yoo, the senior Marine advisor, paid a visit to Monti. I knew he had come a long way to check up on me, and I appreciated his thoughtfulness. We were talking in my hooch when an alert came over the tactical radio: an Army convoy had been ambushed north of Monti. Lt. Kerr and Capt. Bryant, the company commander, were on their way to assist.

I looked at Col. Yoo, who nodded in agreement. Minutes later, Yoo, Bokis, Staff Sgt. Richards, some of the colonel's guys that came with him, a dozen Askars, and I were headed out the gate. We drove a few miles north and stopped at the top of a rise. On our right was the Kunar River. On our left was a towering ridgeline. Two hundred meters to our front was a narrow valley called Dab Khar, a favorite ambush site—steep sides, narrow roadbed. I had fought there before, alongside Staff Sgt. Jeffords.

The valley cut a deep V slice out of the ridgeline. At the bottom of the V, jingle trucks were jammed against each other like a massive traffic accident. Three twelve-wheelers were lying on their sides, burning. Four others, banged up, were parked at crazy angles. Mixed among them were four U.S. Army MRAPs—big armored vehicles—and an armored Humvee.

PKMs and AKs were hammering down on this mess, with little

return fire. It would be crazy to drive into that tangle of vehicles. Bokis was on the MK19 on our truck. He couldn't shoot because of the angles of fire.

Richards stayed in the driver's seat while I advanced on foot by bounds into the wreckage. Our Askars ran forward with us, but their light M16s didn't impress the Taliban machine-gun crew. I was quickly pinned behind a disabled truck. Looking up, I could see the PKM was shooting from a thick stone house two hundred meters upslope. Excited to have a target so close, I fired about five shells from my grenade launcher before my common sense kicked in.

What am I doing? I thought. *I'm outmatched by a machine gun, but there's an Army Humvee sitting next to me with no one in the .50-cal turret!*

I signaled to Capt. Bryant, who had taken shelter behind another jingle truck.

"Why isn't that truck returning fire?" I yelled.

Bryant shrugged, as baffled as I was. Kerr was hunkered down, radioing for air. He was famous for bombing the shit out of insurgents. Gunny Devine and Sgt. Hall were shooting with little effect at the PKM position. I ran over to the Army truck and banged on the hatch. There were bloody handprints all over the door, where the poor Afghan drivers had been banging and begging to be let in.

"Man your .50-cal!" I yelled.

"We're logistics," came the muffled reply. "We don't fight."

Some supply guys can't wait to get into the action, but not this gang. I wasn't worried, though. Wild Man Kerr would soon have air on station.

Bodies were scattered all over the road, all civilians. Lying face-down next to me alongside the Army truck was a skinny teenager in a T-shirt, bleeding from shrapnel in his chest and left arm. With the

American soldiers and Askars putting hundreds of rounds down-range, my M4 wasn't needed. I slung my rifle, wrapped a tourniquet around the kid's arm, picked him up, and carried him back to my Humvee. He had a tracheal deviation and a sucking chest wound. I plunged a decompression dart into the pleural cavity below his third rib and foul-smelling air hissed out his lung. As I was doing this, Specialist Charles Tomeo, the medic in Kerr's platoon, ran up and shoved a plastic tube up the kid's nose to open the airway.

He was a pathetic sight, sprawled on his back in his filthy brown shorts, an orange-tipped needle protruding from above his heart and a plastic stopper shoved up his left nostril. He didn't weigh as much as I ate in a day. His hands and feet were uglier than dirt from his efforts to crawl out of the line of fire. He wasn't old enough to grow a beard, but he had a full shock of black hair. Not a bad-looking kid. Once he was cleaned up at the aid station and had some ice cream, he'd be OK.

I felt good. In fact, I was pumped. I had applied dozens of tourniquets, but this was the first time I had smelled death hiss out. I had saved a human being, a poor, scrawny kid eking out a living by driving a banged-up truck past known ambush sites. Would he eventually join the Taliban and betray an American convoy? I had no idea. Sure, some of the villagers at Ganjigal had been real pricks. But why should I hold that against this kid?

I ran back down the road, hoisted up another wounded truck driver, and carried him back. Then I stopped to check on the skinny kid. I wanted to pat him on the shoulder to make myself feel good for my supposedly wonderful deed. Only he was dead. He had bled to death from the wound to his left arm. The crew in the Army truck had let him bleed out, not five feet away, because he was an Afghan and they were afraid. *Damn it!*

I went back to the wreckage and carried another truck driver back to our truck, where Tomeo bandaged him up. We placed the two wounded in our two trucks, and I put the kid's body on the hood.

When I got back to the messed-up trucks, the enemy fire had slackened because Kerr was directing a Kiowa helicopter overhead. The Afghan drivers were huddled together in a ditch by the river. The ambush had been sprung about ninety minutes earlier. By now they had pissed themselves dry and had nowhere to go. I banged my rifle butt on the Army truck, yelling to the soldiers to open up.

"At least give me some water for those poor bastards!" I shouted.

A sheepish medic got out of the truck with several bottles of water and his medpack and ran over to the ditch. I knelt there, looking at the mud bloodstained from the kid, right beside the truck door.

I banged on the steel door again. It opened a crack.

"Fuck you!" I shouted at the captain inside.

I had placed a firecracker up my ass. I figured the shocked captain would light the fuse as soon as we got back to Monti. Don't ask me why I did it.

By now, Kerr was directing rockets from the Kiowas to provide aiming points for an F-15 and was gleefully bombing the slopes. But we had to unsnarl the traffic mess to get the Army convoy—and my newest buddy, the captain—out of there. Capt. Bryant was yelling at the Afghan drivers to get back in whatever trucks would move. They were looking at him as if he were crazy. Bryant then came up with a brilliant idea.

"Hey, Meyer," he yelled, "get behind the wheel of that big truck, drive it to the edge of the river, and hop out! When they see that, they'll move the others."

I liked Paco Bryant, but there was no way in hell that was happening.

"No, I'm not doing that."

"Why not?"

"Because I'll drown."

"Okay, put a rock on the gas pedal and hop out."

"No. How about *you* get in the truck and *I'll* watch?"

He thought for a moment.

"You got a point," he said. "Get one of those drivers to do it."

I crawled over to a driver and threatened him with my rifle, pointing at the truck. We were still taking some light incoming. He just gestured for me to shoot him, as he preferred that to drowning. I laughed and he smiled back.

So we waited until a big wrecker arrived from Monti that quickly shoved aside the smoking wrecks. That still left a U.S. MRAP stuck in a ditch. Devine and I watched as a soldier hopped down from the wrecker and casually attached chains to the MRAP. We both liked this soldier, a hard worker who grumbled about how roughly grunts treated his beloved trucks.

"Better stay under cover, bro," Devine said.

Instead, the mechanic, with no armor, stood on the road and slowly lit a cigarette.

"No biggie, Sergeant, I got this."

Cigarette dangling from his lip, he signaled to the wrecker with both hands. Mr. Cool from a Camel ad. Very smooth, very much in charge—and very exposed.

Crack!

"I'm hit! I'm hit!"

Mr. Cool was down. We rushed him into the ditch and cut open his right trouser. He'd been drilled through the thigh. The bullet had passed through like a sizzling branding iron.

"Son of a bitch!" he screamed. "Son of a bitch!"

Understandable statement. The pain truly burned and Mr. Cool was definitely hurting. The bullet, though, had missed the femoral artery. A quick tourniquet, a fifteen-minute ride, and he'd be tucked inside clean white sheets, soon on his way to Germany and strawberry ice cream.

At the moment, though, he didn't see the upside. Instead, he was screaming, convinced he was dying. Gunny Devine started to giggle, and I broke out in short snorts. Kerr ran over, took one look at the wound, and hooted.

We weren't heartless. If he had been dying, we would have promised him he was going to live.

As the traffic jam was sorted out, Col. Yoo and I walked back to our Humvee. The dead kid lay on the hood and rather than ride to base with a corpse between us, we wedged the body in the trunk.

Sometimes you laugh, and sometimes you want to cry.

The captain in charge of the logistics convoy did not press charges, although she may have suggested I was too high-strung. The psychologists were keeping an eye on me, calling me in for chats that went round and round.

The weeks crept by. Every now and then, an enemy sniper climbed a few thousand feet above our camp and fired a few rounds. The odds were way low that anyone would be hit, and the camp commander didn't want to place sentries on top of the hill, requiring a three-hour hump each way. A few bullets were like a few falling stars you couldn't do anything about.

Those shots bothered me more than the others. They taunted me. I was sitting in my hooch in October when a high-velocity bullet cracked past the open door. There were shouts in Pashto and the scuffling of running feet. A machine gun in a sentry post fired a short return burst. Then a second bullet snapped by.

I didn't think consciously about it. I just ran outside and hopped in the turret behind a .50-cal. Bokis got behind the wheel and skidded around a corner to give me a clear line of sight. When the sniper took a third shot, I roughly knew his location—a rocky knob about eight hundred meters away. I returned fire, walking a red arc of tracers up to the knob. The sniper stopped shooting, probably hunkered down.

The whole deal pissed me off, being cooped up behind the wire, playing defense and buying time. For what?

A few days later, a farmer showed up on base to complain that bullets had struck his chicken coop. The date matched when I had fired the .50-cal. The farmer claimed he lost five hens.

The civil affairs officer gave him two hundred dollars—forty dollars for each scrawny chicken. The sniper on the farm tries to kill us, and we pay extortion?

Before dropping a shell down a mortar tube, the gunner levels the bubbles on his sight. If he loses the bubbles, then the tube is pointed at a crazy angle. Forty dollars for a chicken? The figure went around and around in my head. After Ganjigal, I was losing the bubble.

Chapter 16

CHEERLEADERS

Standard procedure after an engagement: investigators gather sworn statements. The defeat at Ganjigal generated a lot of paperwork. I wrote a few paragraphs, as did the others. Sgt. Maj. Jimmy Carabello, the top enlisted man in Battalion 1–32, took a personal interest in the battle and reviewed the statements.

I didn't care what happened one way or the other, as long as I stayed far out of his way. Carabello reigned supreme on Joyce. Every soldier in the battalion had a Carabello story. He meted out punishments like ordering a soldier to write a two-thousand-word essay on "Why I should not roll my eyes when my sergeant tells me to do something."

He built a hooch with a veranda where he smoked his cigars in the evening, watching basketball games on the court he'd built a few feet away. He thought the soldiers spent too much time by themselves on their iPods, so he insisted every unit on base field a team.

That wasn't enough. He wanted his soldiers to see real, beautiful cheerleaders. He contacted the USO agent for the cheerleaders for the New England Patriots, who were on tour in the rear. Somehow he persuaded the agent to book an afternoon tea at Joyce with his soldiers. The event went smoothly until a warning via radio intercept. Carabello and the soldiers waved good-bye to the cheerleaders half an hour before rockets slammed into Joyce.

When the sergeant major put his mind to something, you couldn't deflect him. Somehow, after reading the investigation statements, he decided to assemble packets recommending Will Swenson and me for the Medal of Honor. My packet was sent up the Marine channel and Swenson's up the Army channel. I didn't care and neither did Swenson. We were both getting out of the military and we were both furious about Ganjigal.

I'd heard there had been a hasty investigation about Ganjigal that found some shortcomings and "poor battle management" by a captain in the TOC at Joyce. That was a whitewash by higher headquarters, called Joint Task Force 82. It was like saying Lincoln was assassinated because an usher left a theater door unlocked.

My boss, Maj. Williams, had put out the word not to talk to the press. That made sense. I had assumed headquarters would cover for themselves. And why should there be any medals when my team was dead? The hell with it all.

I was up at Monti, far from anybody or anything. My only thought was how to get three hours' sleep so I could function the next day. In return for a forty-dollar chicken, I deserved to shoot somebody.

I walked into my hooch one October day to find a journalist chatting with the other advisors. He had just returned from an operation with Lt. Kerr, who had insisted that he talk with me. We had barely shaken hands when the base took some incoming and I left to check things out. Later that day, I bumped into the writer again.

"One question before I leave," he said. "Any truth to those stories that you were left on your own at Ganjigal?"

"My team would be alive today if we'd gotten artillery," I said.

"You'd tell that to the high command? You'd say that to a general?"

He was straight up about it. I knew that what I said next would be reported high up the chain of command. Maj. Williams—and probably a lot of others—would be furious that I spoke out as a corporal without informing them first. I understood what I was doing before I replied.

"I'd tell that to any general," I said. "We were screwed."

Once I said it, I felt relieved. I had told the truth, the way my dad and the Corps had taught me. Swenson and others had said the identical thing in their statements that were first hidden from public view and later heavily redacted. I knew there would be repercussions for speaking out publicly.

But I didn't expect a few weeks later to be told the Marine general in charge of Afghanistan was flying in to have lunch with me. He was also scheduled to meet privately with Capt. Swenson. I didn't need to be a genius to know that Ganjigal would be the subject.

Lt. Gen. Joseph Dunford was easy to talk with. He had a quiet presence and seemed to know everything about infantry tactics. He was interested in what I thought about dealing with the Askars. I told him that I thought that the American advisors should be infantrymen, and I told him that we were let down at Ganjigal. When we call for fire, we deserve to get it. He didn't ask one word about the investigation and never expressed an opinion, one way or the other. He just listened and left.

I later learned that the Commandant of the Marine Corps, Gen. James Conway, was furious about the superficial nature of the JTF-82 investigation. He believed his Marines had been let down, and he let his feelings be known. Joint Task Force 82 was the command above the advisors and Battalion 1-32. JTF-82's commander, Army Maj.

Gen. Curtis Scaparrotti, ordered a second investigation, jointly conducted by a Marine and an Army colonel.

I wasn't asked to testify. In late November, the two colonels submitted their findings that eventually were published on the Internet with all names blanked out. Gen. Scaparrotti said the lessons learned had been sent to his subordinate commands. Up at Monti, I never heard one lesson.

The fuzziness of the investigations angered me, but I was running on autopilot—training Askars, taking naps, and advising on a few missions outside the wire. My Afghan company—down to fifty-six men—was going through the motions with us advisors. They knew it and we knew it. I got along fine with the Askars, but they were mostly a different bunch. What with Ganjigal and the usual monthly turnover, less than a dozen were left from our high-spirited crew of last summer. It was a different atmosphere with a different group of Afghans. Those who survived Ganjigal were scattered, mostly gone from the army.

We advisors had lost clout because we couldn't get fire support— that was obvious. After Ganjigal, our Afghan battalion commander insisted on joint patrols, with each Askar close enough to grip the belt buckle of an American soldier. My days of hopping behind a .50-cal and driving into a different village each day had come to an end. Except for an occasional foray, we abandoned Dangam.

I did enough chores to keep me busy during the day. At night, the mental barriers of being awake crashed down and the demons crept in. I didn't want to sleep. The Army psychologist I had bumped into down at Joyce kept visiting Monti. She claimed the visits were routine; I knew better. She was talking to some of my friends about me.

She had a quiet way that encouraged men to talk, and some felt I was tightly strung after Ganjigal. I didn't want to discuss my feelings with her.

She sent me twice to a psychiatrist back in Jalalabad. There was this theory called ego depletion. As explained to me, the brain gets depleted after making too many hard decisions. In extreme cases, the mind shuts down and refuses to make decisions. That's called shell shock. That wasn't me. Or the brain takes shortcuts and acts impulsively. That's called reckless behavior. Maybe that was me, a little.

I didn't think my behavior was reckless at Ganjigal, just persistent. In the ambush at Dab Khar, I did curse a captain, and that was maybe reckless. As for blasting that hillside to get a sniper, I was pissed off, and what are you supposed to do when someone is shooting at you?

It's true I didn't feel connected with others. The Askars were smoking hash, jabbering on their cell phones, and wandering around in flip-flops. The American soldiers were playing video games, stuffing themselves at dinner, and laughing too loudly at nothing.

We weren't fighting a war; we were holding a few acres of dirt while the war swirled around outside our barbed wire. There were dushmen in every valley. Drink tea with the villagers? Pay forty dollars for a chicken? We were in Kunar to fight. Let's get it on.

That was my attitude. The psychologist insisted I go back to the States for treatment. No, thanks. As a captain, she had the rank to make her recommendation stick, but she wanted my agreement. So she challenged me: We would play a game of Ping-Pong. If I won, I could stay.

I lost by one point. She was very good, and she really was worried about me and cared about me. I knew that.

It was my turn to go home.

. . .

I flew out from Camp Joyce in December of 2009. Gen. Scaparrotti would tell the press several months later that his command had made progress in eastern Afghanistan, but I didn't see it. Harassing attacks along the paved routes were more frequent. Dangam, where we had guarded the election, was now Taliban territory. The district chief had been killed and the dushmen were getting bolder, lobbing mortar shells and still sniping at Monti. As I was leaving, Battalion 1–32 made yet another effort to win over Ganjigal. Over one hundred American soldiers, supported by gun trucks and helicopter gunships, marched up the village. Declaring they had come in peace, the Americans handed out Korans and prayer rugs. I hope someone prayed for my team.

Chapter 17

OLD HAUNTS

When I got home in December, I felt like I had landed on the moon. Kentucky is pretty much what you think: cheerful bluegrass music like Bill Monroe, rolling countryside, good moonshine, great bourbon, and pretty girls. Greenery, lakes, the creeks and rolling hills, forests, birds, other critters, and all the farms. There's that genuine friendliness that comes with small towns and close-knit families. You don't want to act like an asshole because it will get back to your grandmother by supper.

Something like: "Well, Dakota, I hear you had some words today with that neighbor of Ellen's sister's boy."

Dad, of course, was happy to see me, as were my grandparents, so that was a good feeling. Dad didn't give me a hard time about Ganjigal, and neither did my leatherneck Grandpa. We just didn't talk much about it. It was great seeing my family and friends, but they had their own lives. Everyone around me was excited about football, Christmas, and other normal things; I was looking at the clapboard houses and the cars and thinking, *man—so flimsy. They wouldn't give cover worth shit in a firefight*. It was an exposed feeling. And where were my machine guns? I found my old pistol and kept it around like a rabbit's foot, but I missed my 240s and my .50-cals something awful. It seems weird, I'm sure, but I really just wasn't buying it that there wasn't some enemy about to come over the green hills, and I felt so unprepared—I wouldn't be any good to protect anybody.

I was set to soon go off to Fort Thomas, Kentucky, for PTSD therapy (posttraumatic stress disorder, of course). Maybe that would settle me down and let me get some sleep and stop feeling so depressed and angry at every little thing.

Some guys really go nuts when they come back, and I wasn't in danger of that, but I could feel the kinds of crazy things that maybe got the better of them. As for me, I was a hunter before I went over there, and I was a hunter still—but now I was all nervous about it, like I needed a machine-gun fix. You are over there long enough, and under such constant battle stress, that it resets all your settings way into the red, and they are very hard to set back. The main thing gnawing was that I didn't get my friends out as I had promised. I had spent a good part of my twenty-one years being pretty critical of other people who failed at their responsibilities, and now it was all coming back on me in a big dump truck.

Around Christmas—this was the tail end of 2009—I was sent to the PTSD clinic in Fort Thomas for eight weeks.

Fort Thomas, on the Ohio–Kentucky line, isn't too far north of where we are in Greensburg—about three hours and change.

I was still a Marine. My reenlistment date was coming up, so I wanted to get myself fixed up, good as new. Otherwise, I knew I ought to not re-up, as I was sure they would put me in a desk job if I were still PTSD, and then I would no doubt cuss out some first sergeant and lose my stripes.

There were ten men in my therapy group. We met daily as a group, then individually with the counselors. We wrote down our personal experiences for the eyes of the staff only. We didn't discuss our inner doubts or problems in front of the group—these were all men, and men aren't too chatty about that stuff.

When we were together, we listened to lectures by experts or talked about safe, nonemotional, academic-type subjects. The clinic called it cognitive psychology. Every day, the psychologists urged us to step back and identify why we were experiencing negative emotions. In other words, take a minute to really be conscious of the emotion, instead of just letting it seep in. Don't let your mind stay in neutral. Watch your thoughts.

Refusing to get out of bed, or go to work, or smile at others are all decisions. Find the reasons for those decisions and turn negative feelings into some positive actions. It's not enough to identify why you're feeling bad; it's about having the character to do something positive to take up that space. And don't wallow in your misery, which is just childish self-absorption. That was all good stuff. All I ever need is a good operating manual.

The clinic helped me to not jump to conclusions about people, and to see things through their eyes before I just assumed they were stupid and my enemy.

One soldier in my group had served in Iraq. Two had served in Afghanistan. The other seven were from Vietnam, way back. They were in their sixties.

In a small group, you can't fake whether you've seen combat, even though you're not supposed to talk about it. Over the weeks, you get to know each other. Most of my group had never heard a shot fired, and most of the older guys didn't have steady jobs. Or maybe that was me being judgmental again.

Just the same, money seemed to be the motivating factor for many at the clinic. One man was already drawing $2,600 a month for PTSD. Everyone in the program would leave with some allowance, a tax-free monthly allotment.

Some cases surely require long-term care. I've read about Audie Murphy, the most famous hero of World War II, and all the demons he carried throughout his life. I'm in favor of getting help when it can speed along the healing that time brings. I just didn't like it that some guys were scamming the system. Everybody looked able to go pour cement or something, which is what I figured I'd do if I didn't re-up.

After my two months at the clinic, my enlistment term was, in fact, coming to an end. It didn't take a genius to see it: I'd end up behind a desk. So I chose not to reenlist. I loved the Corps, so it hurt.

Before joining the Corps, I'd had three concussions, mononucleosis, and an operation on my right knee. When I mustered out four years later, I'd added two operations on my right hand, a right rotator cuff operation, a fourth concussion from an RPG, a dislocated shoulder, and two herniated discs from clumsily lifting the dead and wounded. One vertebra had given way in Ganjigal when I picked up an Askar and slipped in the bloody mud under him. I have no idea when the second vertebra went out during the battle. I had that nick in my arm from a bullet or shrapnel, but that hadn't been anything. I was in decent shape for construction work, I figured.

The civilian official in the discharge office glanced at my medical record and pulled out an article about the Ganjigal fight.

I wasn't going to think about it. All I knew was that I was not going to let myself become a mental cripple for life. I was stronger than that. I would always regret not saving my guys, but, as for the people I killed, that is what gave me what little peace of mind I had. They were the enemy. That's what you do to the enemy. That part was not going to upset me. The people who started it are the guilty parties, and I was still figuring that was Mr. Bin Laden. Send him the bill. In fact, that bill was about on the way.

After the PTSD clinic, I returned to Kentucky. It was the winter of 2010 and I warmed myself up by slipping back into hard drinking each night. I wasn't headed to some college where Lt. Johnson would be the military instructor and we'd climb mountains with Staff Sgt. Kenefick and Doc Layton. And I wasn't heading back to finish those bastards above the Kunar River. Dad watched me out of the sides of his eyes.

All of us survivors from Ganjigal were spreading out into the culture. Swenson was up in Seattle somewhere, mustering out of the Army. Staff Sgt. Juan Rodriguez-Chavez, the best Humvee driver who ever lived, was somewhere up near Chicago. Fabayo was in Virginia. Both of them had gone home to a Navy Cross, and they deserved it and more. Swenson and I were up for something, but I didn't believe it would happen or even care—I knew what I had done, and the result was zero.

My friend Hafez, an Afghan, was still stuck at Monti, looking for a way to the States. He had earned entry, for sure, but wasn't getting it. And Monti was deteriorating.

"Am I going to die? Am I going to be all right?" The words were pretty standard, given the blood all over the poor guy. "Am I going to be okay?"

It took me a minute to realize where I was. I had been driving back to the farm from some buddy's house, and I came across a pickup truck on its side. It was like something you would see at Dab Khar. Smoke was coming out from the engine as if it had just taken an RPG.

I pulled over quickly and ran low to the truck, even though there were no bullets hitting around me. I jumped up on the hood and opened the driver's door skyward—it's heavy when the vehicle is on its side like that. There was blood all over the windshield and the interior. The driver, a young guy, was hung up in his seat belt with blood pouring out of his left arm, sliced to the bone. I lifted him out, which was hard, though I didn't feel my back hurting at all, which was good. I got him down to the ground, took off his belt, and cinched it tightly around his biceps to stop the bleeding.

Another driver had stopped and called for an ambulance. It wouldn't come for a good twenty minutes.

He kept asking, "Am I going to be all right?"

"Sure. You're fine. I've seen a lot worse than this. You're fine. You'll be fine." The siren finally. The smell of his blood, the weight of his body in my arms, it was somehow . . . I don't know what it was. It wasn't bad. It was a release. It felt very good to help save someone.

Chapter 18

ALL IN

I shouldn't have read the Ganjigal investigations that came out in 2010. What did I gain by arguing with a computer screen, stewing because as a corporal I hadn't been asked for my opinion? Venting wouldn't change the past. Words, words, words. It seemed to me bureaucrats were pointing fingers in a circle. Since everyone had done something wrong, no one person was held accountable.

That wasn't quite right. There *was* one person accountable, with a straight line of sight to Ganjigal—me. After Rod and I shot those dudes off our truck, a quick dash another quarter-mile would have placed us next to the terraces where my team was. One hundred meters—ten seconds for a runner; thirty seconds for our truck. One quick sprint in.

The investigation had aimed in the wrong direction. I told my team I'd come for them, and I'd pulled off just because of some pressure. I had clutched as badly as those officers back in the TOC at Joyce.

I occasionally called my Army and Marine buddies, and spoke by

Skype a few times with my Afghan friends. I hadn't seen an active-duty grunt in months. Fabayo and Rodriguez-Chavez were due to receive Navy Crosses at the Marine base in Quantico, but I couldn't get enough time off to fly back east. Swenson and I had been recommended for the Medal of Honor. We knew, though, that the award was usually downgraded upon review. When I drank, which was too often, I'd laugh at the absurdity. I had screwed up big-time. My achievement was losing my brothers. The Marine Corps would come to its senses and I'd never hear another word from another devil dog. I had no idea what was in front of me, and I didn't care.

The bottom of the barrel for me came on a country road that is now called the Dakota Meyer Highway in the spring of 2010. After work that night, I visited with some friends and my new best friend, Jack Daniel. By the time I left for home, I had drunk enough liquor to fail a Breathalyzer, but not so much that I was driving erratically.

All I could do was steer and think. I couldn't take a walk, turn on the TV, or read a book to distract my mind. The emptiness of my life was the dark all around me, with nothing to see in any direction.

Four years ago, I had left the farm for adventure and a new beginning. The Corps had shaped me and I had arrived in Afghanistan, confident I'd do well in the combat. Sure enough, up at Monti I had emerged as the Young Gun. Every day brought fun and danger against the backdrop of spectacular mountains. It was fun stuff, shooting thousands of rounds, not losing many people and not seeing the damage you inflicted. There was no weapon I couldn't handle, and my team trusted me to get them out of any hot spot my cockiness put us in.

But when it counted the most, I wasn't with them. They weren't trained to do my job. Gunny Johnson didn't spend every day behind the 240. Staff Sgt. Kenefick wasn't comfortable with weapons or angles of fire. Doc Layton wasn't a fighter, and Lt. Johnson didn't adjust fire missions.

"We aren't worried; we know you'll get us out if anything goes bad, Meyer!"

Well, I didn't, Lieutenant. I was a load of worthless shit, not there when you needed me.

Around three in the morning, I pulled my truck into the driveway of a shop owned by my high school friend Derek Yates, and cut the engine. I turned on the cab light and fished out my cell phone. It wasn't right to burden my dad, but I wanted to connect one last time with someone.

I pecked out a text message to my friends Ann and Toby. They had known me since I was a toddler, but they didn't know me that well, did they? Here I was back where I had started, with an aluminum bracelet with two names on each wrist.

That's what I had done with my life—lost four brothers.

I can't do it anymore, I typed.

I reached into the glove compartment, where I kept my Glock. I always kept a full magazine with a round chambered in the pistol. A Glock doesn't have a manual safety. You pull the trigger, and the weapon fires.

I stuck the gun to my head, squeezed the trigger.

Click.

Nothing. *Nada.* No round in the chamber. As you can imagine, I sat there, quite sobered up and in double shock. Suicide is terminal self-revulsion. I was mixed up, but I knew my team would be disappointed in me. Staff Sgt. Kenefick would give me hell, which was where I would be. Bad ending. That was not going to happen.

But, who had unloaded my pistol? Right on the spot, I knew who had done it. Have I ever talked to that person about it? No.

I put away the pistol and drove home. That night, I experienced no sudden change of direction to my life. I didn't know where I was headed in the future, but I knew quitting wasn't right. Not that night, not ever.

Did the PTSD clinic make a difference in my life? Yes, it did. I'm still here.

I had a good job with a company testing new gear for the military. The work interested me and I was good at it. But at night I was still drinking myself to sleep until Toby and Ann introduced me to Chris Schmidt, the dean of our local college.

Chris was a no-nonsense guy who didn't care about what happened in the past. I lucked out, though; his dad had been a Marine and he had almost volunteered to be a grunt. All he wanted to know was what I was doing today, tomorrow, and the day after that. His solution to problems was to set up a daily routine to overcome them.

He took me into his small bicycle group that hit the roads daily for ten or twenty miles. It wasn't just the exercise; as a group you had to look out for each other on the curves and keep an eye on the traffic. Each rider had to pitch in and was accountable in his own eyes and in the judgment of the group.

I liked that. In some ways, it was like being back at Monti with the team. I had come back to the farm as a loner. That hadn't worked. I wasn't holding myself accountable. In a team, you care about the other guys and don't want to let them down.

. . .

I didn't want to let myself down, either. I was proud that I had served my country and I appreciated all the Marine Corps had done for me. That summer, I took classes at our local college. During one class, a professor told us that we had lost the wars in Iraq and Afghanistan. When I challenged him to explain why, he said we hadn't accomplished anything. "We fought for nothing," he said. "I'm a Vietnam vet, and I know the feeling."

"I served in Iraq and Afghanistan," I said, "and I don't know the feeling. I'm not going to sit here and let you say my guys died for nothing."

The professor believed the Taliban would take over Afghanistan when we left. I didn't look at it in those black-and-white terms. No one can predict how Afghanistan will turn out years from now, and I'll leave it to historians to sort out the mistakes.

We invaded in order to destroy the terrorist network that had murdered three thousand civilians on 9/11. We're safer here in the States than in 2001 because we took the war to the jihadists and didn't play defense inside our own borders. I was fairly worked up by the time the class ended. The professor later apologized, saying he came across stronger than he had intended. I told him I could be a little hard-headed myself.

In August of 2011, a Marine colonel alerted me that the White House was reviewing my award packet and might call me. About two weeks later, the White House operator called. I had switched jobs and was pouring concrete. It was hot, noisy work and I could barely hear. So I asked for a call-back in forty-five minutes. My boss said I could take my lunch break early. I hurried over to the local convenience store, grabbed a Coke, and answered the next call on the first ring.

"Dakota? This is Barack Obama," the president said. "I have just finished reading about the battle and have signed your citation for the Medal of Honor."

For a second, I thought it was a joke. I never expected the president's to be the first voice that I heard, let alone that he would introduce himself by his first name. I stood at attention as I spoke to him. The construction crew had followed me over to the store. I'll never forget their expressions when I gestured to them to quiet down while I talked to the president of the United States.

In September, I flew to Washington. The day before the ceremony, I had half-jokingly said to a White House aide that I'd like to have a beer with the president. When I said that, I didn't mean to be pushy or flippant.

That evening, I sat in a chair outside the Oval Office looking at the Washington Monument and sipping an ale with the most powerful man in the world. It was irrelevant that my political philosophy was quite different from his. He was my commander-in-chief, and he was extremely gracious.

"What's on your mind, Dakota?" the president said.

I told him I didn't have any idea what to do with my life.

His advice was to never stop studying and learning. Education was a lifelong undertaking.

He also observed how he missed the normal things in life, like going to the store to buy shaving cream. He was my commander-in-chief, and he was conveying what was expected of me. I understood his subtle message. I'd have to be extra-careful whenever I drank, or said something when I went out with my friends. I was expected to represent with dignity those who had gone before me, who had given their lives and who had been terribly wounded.

The next afternoon, I returned to the White House for the ceremony. When the president hung that medal around my neck, I felt glum. I couldn't smile and I said nothing. I gave no remarks and avoided the press. As a Marine, you either bring your team home alive or you die trying. My country was recognizing me for being a failure and for the worst day of my life.

In attendance were other Medal of Honor recipients, generals and politicians, friends and relatives, and my comrades-in-arms. Rodriguez-Chavez and his wife were there with his beaming daughters, as were Swenson, Kerr, Bokis, Devine, Jeffords, Skinta—and on and on.

The president hosted us in the East Wing, where kings, prime ministers, ambassadors, and Hollywood stars were normally welcomed. The setting spoke to the history and traditions of America. In the Blue Room hung George P. A. Healy's finest presidential portrait. In the East Room, Gilbert Stuart's painting of George Washington hung above the fireplace. Ben Franklin was on the far wall of the Green Room. The White House seemed almost a living thing, full of power, dignity, and tradition.

Sgt. 1st Class Leroy Petry, awarded the Medal of Honor a few months earlier, showed us how he could rotate his prosthetic right hand. He had lost his hand in Afghanistan throwing back an enemy grenade.

"Why didn't you pitch the grenade away with your left hand?" someone asked him.

"I can't throw lefty," Petry said. "I'd have blown up my buddies and me!"

We all laughed. Here we were—Army and Marine grunts in uniforms with ribbons from a dozen campaigns—drinking beer in rooms accustomed to diplomats and senators. Where else in the world would the head of state welcome into the halls of power, pomp, and history simple warriors who had no political connections or financial riches?

The Marine Commandant, Gen. Jim Amos, and Gen. Joseph Dunford attended the ceremony. Throughout the years after Ganjigal, the Marine Corps leadership had provided consistent support not just to me, but to all who had fought there. The top enlisted man in the Marine Corps, Sgt. Maj. Mike Barrett, twice came to our farm to meet my dad and granddad and to encourage me.

There is no such person as a former Marine. Fifty years after they have left active duty, Marines still sign emails to each other with *S/F—Semper Fidelis*. Always Faithful. Of course we have among us those who fail themselves, their families, and society. The fact remains, though, that the Corps expects every Marine to live by a set of core values. In turn, the Corps keeps its side of the bargain. You cannot ask anything more of an organization than that.

The Medal of Honor, given in the name of the Congress of the United States of America, symbolizes the courage and determination of our entire country. I think if the president hadn't said what he said, I wouldn't have been able to stand it. But I met great people, and still do.

I was in New York City, at the Twin Towers site, Ground Zero, with Gunny Joshua Peterson, someone I knew from my first days in the Corps. We were greeted by hundreds of police, firemen, construction workers, Wall Street guys in suits, city officials, and the families of the fallen.

"Meyer, I can't believe this scene," Gunny Peterson said. "Make sure your ribbons are squared away."

We stood side by side, two grunts in sharply ironed khakis, waving like we had won an election. I thought of my sad, fumbling meetings with the families of Team Monti when I couldn't think of much to say; I was alive and their loved ones were not. Now here I was standing before a monument for three thousand dead.

I saw some big ironworkers in hard hats standing off to one side. When the ceremony ended, they sneaked me onto a work elevator. Up we went to the top of the ride, where we then climbed wooden ladders until we couldn't go any farther and there weren't any guardrails. I stood there looking out at the most beautiful country in the world, trying to make sense of my feelings. This was where it had started, so many good people lost, the people who had been working here, and the people I had known who had not gone blindly into uniform, they had reasoned why—Americans do that—but they had gone ahead to do and to die.

An ironworker handed me a silver marker. I wrote on a girder:

For those who gave all.

Postscript: Swenson

I cannot finish my account without making a special appeal. I'm a Marine sergeant, but I hope the higher-ups in the U.S. Army will listen. On the battlefield, we're all brothers. Rank and service make no difference, and the basic truth is that Capt. Swenson was not treated fairly.

Will Swenson wasn't excitable or impulsive. He wasn't a hard-core jock like Lt. Kerr, primed to take on all comers. Will was your classic laid-back college graduate from the outdoors state of Washington. He sailed, skied, climbed mountains, and traveled the globe. He gave others their space while he went about his job without fuss or drama. Swenson was this quiet, dangerous dude who never said much while calling in fire missions to blow away jihadists. He was the George Clooney type—cool, detached, and lethal when you least expected it.

Swenson had been infuriated by the lack of fire support at Ganjigal. He had signed statements blasting the rules of engagement and the attitudes of higher headquarters.

"I get these crazy messages saying that, 'hey!, brigade is saying you can't see the target from your OT [observer-target line],'" he wrote. "Brigade, you're in Jalalabad. Fuck you. I am staring at the target . . ."

"Fuck you," to his high command. For Swenson to blow up like that in a sworn statement, you knew the frustration came from deep

in his heart. He felt he had crossed the line with those high above him.

"I'm still sleeping in my [sleeping] bag," Swenson said a few weeks after he testified. "I expect to be kicked out."

Hundreds of soldiers and officers at all levels knew that Swenson had been nominated for the Medal of Honor. Gen. Dunford met with Swenson at Joyce in mid-November to thank him for his courage. Dunford's schedule had been coordinated at all the senior commands. Yet no Army general flew to Joyce to meet with Swenson.

Lt. Col. Mark O'Donnell signed the recommendation for the Medal of Honor in December of 2009. The form, together with thirty-five supporting appendices, was sent to the 4th Infantry Brigade, the next higher headquarters. The brigade commander signed the form, added a handwritten endorsement, and in January sent it to the Combined Joint Task Force, or CJTF-82, commanded by Maj. Gen. Curtis Scaparrotti.

JTF-82 was an infantry command, where performance in battle is everything. A nomination for the Medal of Honor was a huge happening. If you join the Army or Marine Corps, you obey its rules and trust the institution to apply the same rules to everyone—corporals, captains, and generals. Strict regulations prescribed the chain of custody and signatures required for the Medal of Honor.

Army Maj. Gen. Jeffrey Schloesser, who commanded RC-East in 2008, nominated three soldiers for the Medal of Honor. "The process of nominating," he said, "is truly one of the most important things a commander does in combat."

In 2009, Maj. Gen. Scaparrotti took command of RC-East, and unfortunately Swenson's nomination was eventually lost. This occurred during a period of intense scrutiny into CJTF-82. In addition to the investigation into the events at Ganjigal, three other investigations were under way regarding CJTF-82's combat procedures. In May of 2009, the insurgents had overrun an outpost north of Joyce called Bari Alai. Three American and two Latvian soldiers had died, leading to an investigation by the television correspondent Dan Rather. In July, Battalion 1–32 was sent north to fight in a fishbowl called Barge Matal, leading to questions about operational decision-making. Then followed the ambush at Ganjigal, with an initial investigation that infuriated the Marine Corps. In October, an outpost named Keating was overrun, with a loss of eight U.S. soldiers. Another investigation was opened. Then in November, a second investigation into Ganjigal revealed serious command errors.

Swenson symbolized Ganjigal, and Ganjigal conveyed the wrong message: failure to support advisors, failure to provide artillery support, failure to deliver timely air support, et cetera.

In the midst of all those investigations, Gen. Scaparrotti's headquarters lost the one-inch-thick packet recommending the Medal of Honor. The processing guidelines were crystal-clear, with no ambiguity. Plus, at the end of each calendar year, the orders log and a specific form had to be uploaded into the Army electronic archives. CJTF-82 did not follow those steps. Swenson's nomination for the award held most sacred in the military disappeared without a trace. The packet had vanished into thin air, forgotten by everybody in the chain of command.

When Swenson returned to the States in the winter of 2010, he was assigned to Fort Lewis in Washington, where the overall commander was Scaparrotti, who had been promoted to lieutenant general. Several briefings for Scaparrotti included the name of Will Swenson as the author. But the general never called Swenson in for a chat.

Swenson had been wrong to fear that the Army would fire him.

Instead, he served out the remainder of his term and resigned quietly. The Marine Corps awarded each of my four fallen comrades a posthumous Bronze Star with combat V. Army Sgt. 1st Class Westbrook received no such combat V, and Swenson's career as a grunt was over.

In August of 2010, Col. Daniel Yoo, my senior advisor commander, on two occasions informed the Marine Central Command about the recommendation for Swenson. Yoo wrote that he was noting this "for the record." This was a subtle way of suggesting that Central Command ask what had happened to the missing award packet.

In April of 2011, Gen. George Casey, the chief of staff of the Army, was notified by an unofficial back channel that "Swenson received no award. This has caused disquiet among those who were at Ganjigal." Casey alerted the senior Army staff to begin a search for Swenson's lost file. A senior Army staffer in Afghanistan conducted an informal investigation, found the lost recommendation, and resubmitted it in August.

The overall commander in Afghanistan, Gen. John R. Allen, took up the chase in August, requesting Swenson's file be brought to him. Lt. Gen. Scaparrotti was back in Afghanistan as the Corps commander. His staff sent Allen a duplicate packet of the original recommendation. Allen immediately endorsed the recommendation and graciously wrote a letter of apology for the delay to Swenson. Asked why he did this when he had not been in command two years earlier and had no responsibility for the oversight, Allen replied, "Because it was the right thing to do."

Allen sent the file to Gen. James N. Mattis, who commanded the Central Command. Mattis was a tough grunt famous for once quipping, "Be the hunter, not the hunted." He compared the statements in my packet with those attesting to Swenson. Most were identical or highly similar. He handwrote a strong endorsement, stating that he had no doubt that Swenson deserved the Medal of Honor. He sent his endorsement to the Army chain of command in the States.

Finally, after a lapse of two years, the Army as an institution seemed poised to do the honorable thing. I waited a few months for word that Swenson would be recognized. But no one in the Army called Will.

So in November of 2011, I decided to send my objections directly to the White House. It was unjust that I had stood at attention before our commander-in-chief without Capt. Swenson at my side. Below is a condensed version of the email that I sent to Lt. Gen. Douglas Lute, U.S. Army, the senior officer on the National Security Council staff. Lute had the reputation of being a straight shooter.

> *Dear General Lute,*
>
> *I would like my testimony about the valor of Capt. Will Swenson to be received by the proper authorities. At Ganjigal, it was Swenson that I heard repeatedly calling for fires. It was clear he was running the show and was the centerpiece for command and control in a raging firefight that never died down.*
>
> *Our group consisted of Swenson, Fabayo, Rodriguez-Chavez, me, and a brave Afghan interpreter named Hafez. From 0745 on, we were together. Swenson tried to get that platoon to help us. When I couldn't get the body [of Dodd Ali] into the truck, Swenson hopped out and completed the task. We made several trips in looking for my advisor team, bringing out some wounded and dead each time.*
>
> *Swenson controlled all the helos. He picked out the targets and kept situational awareness, radioing cardinal directions and distances. Not everyone can do that when bullets are continuously hitting the sides of your truck.*

Swenson was not the senior commander; he just took over and everyone deferred to him. To the extent that anyone was in charge on that chaotic battlefield over the course of six or seven hours, it was Captain Will Swenson.

Bottom line: I would not be alive today if it were not for Will Swenson!

Sincerely, Dakota L. Meyer

General Lute was very courteous. He assured me he had looked into the matter and sent my email to the proper authorities in the Army. When no one contacted me for my testimony, I chose to believe that the Army had thoroughly investigated Capt. Swenson's conduct during the battle and had no need of further testimony. Throughout the summer of 2012, the Army continued with its internal reviews.

I am sure the Army will eventually reach the right conclusion. Capt. William Swenson fully deserves the Medal of Honor for his gallant leadership and valor. Only when that happens will fairness and accountability have prevailed after Ganjigal.

Epilogue

BING WEST

Dakota looked like he was going to a funeral when I met him in a hotel lobby near the White House two years after Ganjigal. His family, friends, and battle buddies were chatting in amiable groups, occasionally waving in our direction. He nodded somberly, responding civilly to a situation he wanted to avoid. He looked around, bemused.

"Can you believe this is happening?" he said.

I had met Cpl. Meyer at Combat Outpost Monti a few weeks after the Ganjigal battle. I was embedded for a second time with Battalion 1–32, and Lt. Jake Kerr insisted that I meet the "pit bull." I included a chapter about Ganjigal in a book called *The Wrong War*, then turned to other writing assignments.

A year later, Dakota asked if I would write a book with him. I demurred, explaining that an agent could provide him with many qualified writers. That wasn't the point, Dakota said; he wanted a grunt to deliver his message.

"I can write about battle," I said. "But I don't want to hear about your sex life."

"Don't worry," he said. "You're too old to remember what that is."

· · ·

Hmm. I had written my first book, *Small Unit Action in Vietnam,* in 1966. While that had been several decades before Dakota was born, it wasn't exactly as long ago as World War I. Since then, I've been in battles in jungles, villages, deserts, and mountains and written seven books about combat that shared one trait: chaos. Every retelling of battle is a description of confusion.

Ask a dozen players to reconstruct a football game and you will get a dozen differing accounts. Imagine, then, the confusing recollections after a battle. The Ganjigal battle, given its ferocity and the antagonisms toward the staffs in the rear, had a number of contradictions in the footnotes citing the sworn statements of the participants.

There is agreement, however, about the overall narrative. I was not present at the battle, although I had embedded several times in the Ganjigal region and knew many of the soldiers and advisors. This book is based upon hundreds of hours of discussions with Dakota. I've also talked with other participants and have pored over dozens of witness statements and investigations. The quotes are illustrative and not the actual words used in the fight. These are his words and expressions. This is Dakota's account from start to finish.

In its ferocity, valor, treachery, and bungling, Ganjigal was extraordinary. The battle resulted in thirteen friendly fatalities, two investigations, two reprimands for dereliction of duty, one Medal of Honor and the "loss" of the recommendation for a second Medal of Honor. A writer imposes coherence upon chaos by selecting a point of view and developing themes that tie the narrative together. The focus of this book is the character growth of Dakota Meyer. His story stands as a metaphor for the war. It illustrates three themes: a frustrating war, a misplaced strategy, and the grit of the American warrior. Let's look at each of the three.

First, the frustrating war has no end point. By giving the Taliban a sanctuary, the Pakistani generals have ensured that the war will go on indefinitely. Our soldiers are fighting only so that Afghan soldiers can take over the fight. In Vietnam, I patrolled in a dozen villages like Ganjigal, where the farmers were inscrutable and enemy without uniforms sprang ambushes. Afghanistan is a similarly elusive and maddening war, where the host government is unreliable and tribal loyalties are suspect.

That medieval culture defied reshaping by our policymakers. President Obama called Afghanistan "the good war" and doubled the number of troops, followed by ordering a withdrawal. Our troops have taken the war to the enemy and placed the Islamic terrorists on the defensive. That's about as much as can be done. Wars fought for fuzzy objectives are not guaranteed to succeed.

Such irregular wars will repeat regularly. Because we are a nation that pursues success, we are frustrated by such ambiguity. We don't want to divide our country, as in the Vietnam era, when there was an unpopular draft. That is why we have an all-volunteer force. We need warriors like Dakota who fight willingly when our elected commander-in chief gives the order.

A second theme that emerges is strategic overreach at senior operational levels. Our generals insisted that democratic nation-building was the only viable military strategy. Grunts like Swenson and Meyer knew nation-building was too ambitious. A thousand years of culture, religion, and traditions separated us from the tribes.

No outpost was ever established in the valley of Ganjigal. Qari Zia Ur-Rahman, the Taliban commander during the battle, was a hard-core Islamist dedicated to winning. He often boasted of his victory at

Ganjigal and circulated pictures of the equipment taken from the bodies of Team Monti. Despite a $350,000 bounty, Rahman has remained in command of Kumar for years without being betrayed, a disturbing indicator of the tribal loyalties and the balance of power along the 1,500-mile border. In ten years, U.S. leaders failed to develop a method for changing the nature of the Islamic mountain tribes.

We should have deployed thousands of advisors like Dakota to train Afghan soldiers, and then left. Instead, our generals focused on winning the hearts and minds of tribesmen hurtling headlong into the ninth century. This resulted in top-down rules of engagement that paralyzed mid-level staffs like the TOC at Joyce. The ROE "expressly prohibited" air or artillery strikes unless the ground commander had "positively identified enemy forces within a residential compound."

Not even the Kiowa pilots flying ten feet above the houses could "positively" identify enemy who didn't wear uniforms. Capt. Kaplan, who had been on the southern outpost (OP), told the investigators that the rules of engagement shielded the villagers who were helping to kill Americans.

"The ROE protects civilians at the cost of American lives," he said. "I understand this to be within the spirit of COIN (counterinsurgency), and the intent of the Commander, but it does not adequately account for situations in which there may be no non-hostile actors."

With the villagers aiding the Taliban, who was not hostile? Using stronger language, Fabayo echoed Kaplan's condemnation.

"I have never heard of a rule that would not allow you to fire on a house," Fabayo said. "They always teach you that you always have the right to defend yourself."

Gen. Scaparrotti had promised, "our fallen heroes and Gold Star families, you'll not be forgotten." The angry Gold Star families, however, believed that the investigation was a cover-up for the higher-ups. Swenson was so furious that he mocked the senior staffs for playing video games.

"The ground commander is calling in that mission because he feels that he needs it," Swenson testified. "It's not JAG [lawyers'] responsibility to interject to say, 'Hey, we are concerned that you're going to hit a building . . . I am concerned with saving as many lives as I can . . . When I am being second-guessed by somebody that's sitting in an air-conditioned TOC, well hell, why am I even out here in the first place? Let's just sit back and play Nintendo . . . I am not a politician. I am just the guy on the ground asking for that ammunition to be dropped because it's going to save lives."

The senior command had issued rules of engagement without addressing who had the authority to make the final decision. Maj. Williams believed he was only an advisor, and that the Afghan major, who didn't know how to call in fire, was in charge. Swenson believed he had the right to assume the role of ground commander and make the decisions. The staff back at the ops center in Joyce overrode his fire requests. Authority was diffuse, and no single person was held accountable. What a mess!

Gen. Colin Powell, widely admired as chairman of the Joint Chiefs of Staff in the early 1990s, had a strong opinion about command decision-making. "The commander in the field is always right and the rear echelon is wrong, unless proved otherwise," he wrote. "In my experience, the people closest to the problems are often in the best position to see the solutions. The key here is to empower and not be the bottleneck."

. . .

The third—and most important—theme of the book is grit. Under fire, some men put their faces in the dirt, most shoot back, and a very few charge forward. Dakota's story was remarkable for its dogged aggressiveness. Most acts of bravery occur at a single point in time; Dakota rushed toward death, not once, not twice, but *five* times. Between each attack, he had time to reconsider. Once inside the wash, he repeatedly left the truck for so long that Rodriguez-Chavez several times thought he had been killed. Can you imagine dodging bullets to carry back wounded Afghan soldiers, or leaning over the side of a truck to shoot a man, or pounding in a man's face with a rock?

The Medal of Honor pays no attention to rank, education, or background; it symbolized the American fighting spirit. In concept, Dakota understood that the Medal honored the sacrifice of his comrades. At night, though, monsters crept out of his closet. When he sipped a beer with his commander-in-chief, I knew what he eventually blurted out.

"You either get them out alive, or you die trying," he said on *60 Minutes*. "If you didn't die trying, you didn't try hard enough."

Dakota believed he was accepting an award for failure, a burden he no doubt will carry with him for the rest of his life. But had he not driven off the jihadists who swarmed his truck, the medevac helicopter would have been a sitting duck—Fabayo tried to wave off the chopper—and the escape route out of the valley sealed off, turning a tragedy into a full-blown catastrophe. Intellectually, I think he understands that. Emotionally, he focuses on what he is convinced that he did not do—save his brothers.

What drove him forward? Was he shaped by his upbringing in a farming community with traditional American values, or by his tough training as a Marine sniper?

His nature led him to charge into the fire. That instinct sprang from a Kentucky upbringing that stressed determination. *Finish the game.*

Regardless of his grit, in that valley he was a dead man, had he not been so expert with a variety of weapons. He wouldn't have stood a chance had he not been able to handle a .50-cal, a 240 machine gun, a grenade launcher, and an M4 rifle without ever thinking. He had the muscle memory of a professional athlete, an instinct acquired by thousands of hours of practice. Four years of Marine training and discipline had nurtured his skills.

So was it nature or nurture that drove him forward into the fire? In the case of Dakota, it was both—testimony to the invincibility of the American warrior.

Acknowledgments

For a long while, I tried to forget about Ganjigal. When that didn't work out so well, I decided to go through what had happened to me, piece by piece. I had written some stuff when I was up at Monti, mostly about my team and the battle. Later, I talked into a recorder for hours—about growing up, being a Marine, the ambush at Ganjigal, and coming to grips with life after the battle. The pictures I had taken and the dozens of statements in the investigations were a big help. The hardest work was going over draft after draft, sorting out what happened when.

I regret that I cannot share the names of several of the Afghans who stood by us Americans in those moments of agony. Intellectually, I understand it was their duty to defend their country. Emotionally, though, I was deeply touched by those who fought in conditions beyond the call of duty. The sad part is that I cannot divulge some names because those Afghans would be placed on a Taliban hit list inside their own country. How's that for irony?

Bing and I would also like to thank the many who took the time to talk with us, including Lt. Col. Ishaq Tamkeen, Lt. Col. Dan Yaroslaski, Capt. Ademola Fabayo, Capt. Ray Kaplan, Lt. Jake Kerr, Gunny Kevin Devine, Sgt. Maj. Jimmie Carabello, Lt. Col. Mark O'Donnell, Brig. Gen. Daniel Yoo, Capt. Michael Harrison, Gunny Mike Skinta, Gunny Joshua Peterson, Staff Sgt. Chuck Bokis, Staff Sgt. Juan

Rodriguez-Chavez, Hafez, CWO Yossarian Silano, Dean Chris Schmidt, my dad, Big Mike Meyer, Ann and Toby Young, my grandfather and grandmother Mema and Pepa, my teachers Mrs. Tana Rattliff and Heather Moss, and coaches Mike Griffiths, Toby Curry, and Will Hodges.

Our editor, Will Murphy, Mika Kasuga, Dennis Burke, and our agent, Sloan Harris of ICM, labored mightily through several drafts to impose an understandable narrative on a confused battle.

The comradeship and help I have received from the Marine Corps as an institution have been tremendous. I would especially like to thank the Commandant, Gen. Jim Amos, and also Gen. Joseph Dunford, Sgt. Maj. Mike Barrett, Lt. Col. Chris Hughes, Punch Haynes of the Marine Corps—Law Enforcement Foundation, and Owen West of the Marine Corps Scholarship Foundation.

The Marines who had the most influence on my life were: Gunny Soto-Rodriguez, Gunny Peterson, Gunny Duprey, Gunny Rich, Gunny Nunn, Sgt. Rooney, Sgt. Pape, Sgt. Kreitzer, Sgt. Smith, Staff Sgt. Gavin, Sgt. Moenich, CWO Skinta, Cpl. Morin, and Cpl. Coggins.

I would also like to thank the family members who stood next to me when I returned home: my brother Tim, uncle Mark, aunt Cindy, Matt and Jennie Meyer, Troy, Steven, Casey Danzinger, and Austin Nettleship. My friends who were always there: Mike Staton, Dean Adams, Jeff, Vikki, Blake, and Randy Hatcher, Mike and Amy Mitchum, Levi Burton, Randy Hadeed, Reed Bergman, Keith Delucia, Maurice Freedman, Gary and Kevin Vernon, Adam Weinbrenner, Ben Madden, Joe Mangione, Dana, Ray, Diane, Ryan, Jay, and Sabrina Benedict, Andy Olson, Clint Walker, Jeff Suratt, and Monica Johnson. One look at those names and you can see that I am truly blessed.

And thank you to all who have donated to the Dakota Meyer Scholarship (www.dakotameyer.com). So far we have raised more than one million dollars for the education of the children of the wounded.

Every word in this book is what I remember to the best of my ability. I've been over this book time and again, separately with Bing, with our editor, Will Murphy, with Dean Schmidt, and with Toby and Ann. Will Swenson was also a great help. Perhaps writing the narrative will help me come to terms with what happened. I hope so.

To the families of Lt. Mike Johnson, Staff Sgt. Aaron Kenefick, Doc Layton, and Edwin Johnson, I offer my everlasting and profound regret. The Marine Corps teaches you not about trying, but about doing, and I didn't get there in time. I will forever miss my team.

Appendix 1

GANJIGAL TIMELINE
(EVENTS OF SEPTEMBER 8, 2009)

TIMELINE

0100–0400	Numerous enemy groups moving toward Ganjigal.
0330	Embedded training team (ETT) 2–8 and Askars link with Highlander 5 and border police; in a file of vehicles, they turn off main road and head east into Ganjigal Valley.
0400	One mile inside the valley, they stop at operational release point (ORP); they dismount and proceed on foot.
0530	Afghan National Army (ANA) observation post to north above the wash leading into Ganjigal (Marines on the outpost [OP] were Miller and Valadez).
0530	Kaplan and Cpl. Norman and twelve ANA set up southern OP with a 240 Golf machine gun.

0530	1–32 scout-sniper team called Shadow 4 on OP farther back on south side, 1,200 meters away—too far to apply direct fire, but in excellent position to relay radio messages from the valley to the tactical operations center (TOC) at Joyce.
0530 (0100 Zulu)	Contact reported to TOC of Battalion 1–32 at Camp Joyce.
0530	Lt. Johnson four-man party (Team Monti) 100 meters in front of TAC/Command Group when firing begins; Swenson runs 100 meters forward to join Lt. Johnson's TAC (tactical command post) and calls suppression artillery fire.
0537	Shadow (Staff Sgt. Summers and Staff Sgt. Alvarez) reports first 120-millimeter mission KE 3070.
0545	ANA soldiers disperse among terraces.
0545	Rodriguez-Chavez on radio hears Lt. Johnson tell Fabayo he needs fires to get out of a house.
0545	Meyer's requests to enter wash are denied via Fox 7 (Valadez radio relay).
0546	Call for fire KE 3345.
0547	Meyer, Valadez, and Rodriguez-Chavez in discussions.
0550	Splash KE 3345 four HE 120s fire from Joyce; Garza testified this was effective fire.
0551	Swenson requests air—told air is coming in fifteen mikes (minutes).
0556	Call for fire KE 3365.
0557–0630	Kaplan calls/relays seven smoke missions; denied because too close to civilians.

0600	Splash 3070 four HE 155s from Asadabad (A-Bad).
0600	Staff Sgt. Kenefick tries to give grid.
0600	Meyer and Rodriguez-Chavez disobey orders and drive toward the battle.
0600	TOC via Shadow again assures Highlander (Swenson) that CCA (close combat aviation) helo support is "fifteen minutes away."
0605	Splash KE 3365 eight HE 120s; Garza testified this had no effect, even when adjusted.
0605	Swenson and Fabayo agree to pull back.
0610	Meyer and Rodriguez-Chavez signal to five ANA soldiers to get into their truck.
0615	Staff Sgt. Lantz, NCO in charge in TOC at Joyce (Hammer), contacts 7–17 Cav (Pale Horse) in direct support of 4/4 BCT in Op Lethal Storm in Shuriak Valley, 5 kilometers to the north of Ganjigal; Lantz requests re-tasking two OH-58 (Kiowas) Scout Weapons Team (SWT) 1.
0615	TOC directs Dog platoon to prepare to go forward.
0616	In TOC, joint terminal attack controller (JTAC)–qualified Tech Sgt. Matzke asks officer on watch to declare an air TIC (troops in contact) to bring in fixed-wing CAS (close air support), but request is denied.
0618	Swenson calls for fire for smoke at grid 902 515 to cover withdrawal; denied.
0620	7–17 ops center denies Lantz's request on procedural grounds "not routed through brigade";

	7–17 declares SWT 1 is "in support of higher-priority mission."
0620	Villagers join attack.
0625	Shadow reports to TOC that the ANA (Askars) are under fire from the north, east, and south—eight to ten enemy positions with rocket-propelled grenades, PKM machine guns, and mortars deployed in a horseshoe around Ganjigal village. (Note: battle captain [senior watch officer] was located in southwest corner of TOC, could not hear radio transmissions, and relied on others to tell him what was said.)
0625	Command Group in wash falling back toward the west.
0630	Maj. Williams and Maj. Talib request help; Talib calls Afghan battalion commander via cell phone.
0630	TOC orders Dog to move forward; platoon leader complains he has no grid for link-up or LOA.
0633	Will Swenson throws grenade and kills three insurgents in ANA gear.
0634	TOC requests CCA via Task Force Pale Horse 7–17 ops center; again, this creates hesitation because it is out of the normal request pattern, but 4/4 Brigade Ops Center intervenes and backs up 1–32 request.
0635	Shadow reports Dog platoon breaking down its TCP (traffic control point) to move to support.
0635	Command Group forced to fall farther back; reporter does not move with the group.
0639	Splash white phosphorus four rounds from 120

	mortars to east of village, too far away to provide concealment for Team Monti.
0639	TOC denies any more artillery support, citing garbled communication, lack of situational awareness on part of Shadow, and incomplete fire mission procedures; no more arty fired until 1615 of that same day.
0644	Swenson sends his initials for polar fire mission—denied; Capt. Ray Kaplan doing same.
0650–0700	Westbrook hit; Garza and reporter, who has rejoined the group, help him; Garza concussed; Afghan interpreter killed; Williams nicked; Swenson applies first aid to Westbrook.
0655	Fabayo and Swenson continue to cover short retreat sprints over dirt furrows; Lt. Rhula shot in groin/upper thigh.
0700	TOC battle captain asks Tech Sgt. Matzke, a JTAC, what CAS is available, but tells Matzke not to open air TIC.
0702	Last comm with Team Monti.
0703	Swenson alerts Shadow he will send nine-line helo medevac for Westbrook.
0707	Shadow relays Swenson's request to TOC.
0709	Dog platoon reports its limit of advance to TOC.
0710	CCA approved by Task Force Mountain Warrior (brigade level).
0710	Shadow takes fire from the south, calls for immediate suppression fire mission 957 493 1 kilometer to their rear on higher ground.
0715	Swenson alerted that helos are inbound.

0720	Werth/Hooker investigation: Team Monti estimated as "likely dead" by this time.
0720	Shadow fire mission request is posted in TOC.
0721	A-Bad PTDS (blimp cameras) reports muzzle flashes at 983 511.
0723	Two Kiowas test-fire their guns into Kunar River as they approach Ganjigal.
0725	Dog platoon ASV (30,000-pound Army security vehicle) has slipped off road; platoon leader leaves Meyer, returns to trail to CCP, and calls for a wrecker to come forward from Camp Joyce.
0730	A-Bad PTDS reports enemy at 983 511.
0730	Swenson (Highlander 5) directs Kiowas that provide covering fire as Command Group pulls back.
0738	Chosin TOC receives nine-line medevac request for two wounded in action (WIA).
0739	Dog platoon reports limit of advance at 969 519.
0740	Fabayo sees Rodriguez-Chavez and Meyer pull in front of Command Group to provide suppressive fire.
0745	Command Group is out of the wash, away from direct fire.
0745–0845	Pale Horse delivers ten close combat attacks (CCAs).
0746	Pale Horse (Kiowas) make contact with Meyer.
0746	TOC does not respond to Kiowas on Common Air-to-Ground (CAG) net; Pale Horse decides to take his directions from Highlander 5 (Swenson) and Fox 3-3 (Meyer).

0747	Senior officer in TOC talks directly to neither Shadow 4 nor Dog platoon, although both are in direct voice communications with TOC.
0748	Shadow repeats request for air medevac at 953 518—one U.S. (Westbrook) and one ANA.
0749	Shadow again requests medevac.
0750	Dog platoon reports ASV rolled over twice and landed on its wheels at 954 518; no injuries.
0755	Dog platoon reports green on all personnel.
0800	SWT 1 (Kiowas) breaks station over Meyer to escort medevac.
0800	Capt. Richardson takes over as watch officer in ops center, but is junior to battalion commanding officer (XO) and S-3, who are both in TOC.
0800	Swenson puts out air panels at CCP; Fabayo does the same.
0810	Shadow no longer taking fire.
0810	Dog platoon reports mass casualty situation—six killed in action (KIA), ten WIA; sets up mass casualty evacuation point.
0812	Rodriguez-Chavez and Meyer are swarmed inside wash by about ten enemy.
0822	Blackhawk lands under fire to evacuate critically wounded Sgt. Westbrook.
0824	Pale Horse Kiowas leave to refuel at A-Bad.
0830	Swenson and Fabayo drive into wash as Meyer and Rodriguez-Chavez drive out.
0830–0910	Swenson, Fabayo, Meyer, Rodriguez-Chavez, and Hafez make repeated short runs into wash, picking up dead and wounded.

0833	Dog platoon reports soldier has rib and pelvic pains from rollover of ASV.
0838	Three wounded Askars arrive at Joyce in a Ranger.
0845–1135	Two Kiowas continuously on station along the wash; expend 1,800 rounds of .50-cal and fifteen HE rockets.
0845	No U.S. quick reaction force (QRF) has departed Joyce; XO later said he didn't keep a QRF on alert.
0846	Afghan Army at Joyce dispatches a QRF.
0848	From Asmar, 12 kilometers north, Afghan Border Police dispatch a QRF.
0856	Dog platoon ASV self-recovered.
0900	Col. George, brigade commander, departs Jalalabad Air Base, picks up Afghan 2nd Brigade commander, Col. Asval.
0905	Three more Askar wounded sent by Ranger to Joyce.
0910	Rodriguez-Chavez and group drive to ORP and get a truck with a working machine gun.
0910	Swenson asks Dog platoon to help him; platoon leader responds that he has three times asked TOC to send a wrecker and Humvees, and has been told to remain in place.
0911	Swenson curses platoon leader.
0915	Meyer talks with Garza and Williams at CCP.
0921	Dog reports indirect fire being walked toward their position near CCP and so are moving back.
0928	Dog reports four U.S. advisors and an Afghan squad are missing.

0930	Tech Sgt. Matzke on own initiative calls 4/4 Brigade TOC to request an air TIC to receive fixed-wing air support.
0930	Williams, Garza, and reporter leave for Camp Joyce.
0935	Pale Horse (Silano) orders Meyer not to walk alone back into wash; Meyer halts, with Pale Horse hovering above him.
0937	Another platoon from Dog and a platoon from Alpha/Attack Co. start toward Ganjigal Valley.
0938	Swenson, Rodriguez-Chavez, Hafez, and Fabayo drive from ORP to CCP, pick up Meyer, and drive back into wash, with Pale Horse Kiowas in extremely close support (fifteen feet over their heads).
0945	Swenson and Meyer work with Kiowas to spot and retrieve Askars, who are placed in Afghan vehicles.
0948	Two F15Es are on station (Dude 01) but refuse to drop bombs because they cannot identify targets.
0955	Col. George (TF Mountain Warrior) and Col. Asval (ANA brigade commander) arrive TOC at Joyce; neither proceeds forward to battlefield.
1000	Afghan Army QRF arrives Ganjigal and follows Swenson/Meyer Humvee up wash; no U.S. forces follow.
1005	U.S. Attack and Dog platoons link up but stay off the battlefield.
1012	Another platoon from Dog arrives at Joyce.
1015	UAV on station.

1045	Afghan border police QRF arrives Ganjigal and joins battle.
1047	Pale Horse Kiowas heavily engaging Taliban (AAF—Anti-Afghan Forces) at grid 983 511.
1050	CJTF ops center contacts ISAF Joint Command (IJC Corps Command) to declare "personnel recovery"; DUSTWUN (Duty Status—Whereabouts Unknown); Special Operations forces en route to Ganjigal.
1056	Williams and Garza arrive at Joyce.
1100	Special Operations Force Blackhawk on station at Ganjigal; encounters heavy fire when throwing out smoke; cannot land a recovery team.
1110	Pale Horse hovers over trench line and identifies Team Monti.
1120	Meyer and Swenson find four U.S. (Team Monti) and one Afghan KIA.
1202	Meyer and Hafez arrive at Joyce with two bodies.
1220	Meyer and Bokis prepare the bodies for movement to the rear.
1300	Sgt. Maj. Carabello tells Meyer to wash the blood from his face.
1335	Four bodies of Team Monti flown from Joyce.
1400	Eight bodies of Afghan soldiers driven to A-Bad or kept at Joyce for relatives to claim for burial.
1416	Swenson, Kaplan, and seven Marine advisors arrive back at Joyce.
1530	Special Forces prepare to sweep Ganjigal.
1600	Meyer prepares two Askars for burial, visits the

wounded Askars, and eats dinner on the roof
with Hafez and several Afghan soldiers.

FRIENDLY FORCE

Thirteen Marine and two Army advisors plus Capt. Kaplan, plus sixty
Afghan National Army and thirty Afghan border police, plus one
U.S. Army platoon in reserve, plus sixteen U.S. Army scout-sniper
soldiers on northern observation post.

VERSUS

Forty-five to sixty enemy, mostly from Pakistan, with some aid from
about a hundred villagers.

LOCATIONS AND CALL SIGNS

South OP (Kaplan—Chosin 2, Cpl. Norman—Fox 2): grid XD 970
516.

Scout-sniper South OP (Sgt. Summers—Shadow 4): grid 954 510.

North OP (Miller, Valadez—Fox 7): grid 970 523.

In the valley (Williams—Fox 6, Fabayo—Fox 3, Garza—Fox 9,
Swenson—Highlander 5, Meyer—Fox 3–3, Rodriguez-Chavez—
Fox 3–2): center grid 972 520.

Ganjigal village: grid 978 520.

Schoolhouse: grid 973 517.

CCP: grid 955 519.

ORP: grid 949 521.

Team Monti: found at grid 974 519.

Reported enemy positions (thirteen) at grids 972 517, 982 522, 981 521, 973 516, 971 516, 972 518, 975 516, 968 526, 975 520, 985 490, 983 532, 975 521, 957 493 (this indicates the enemy were mobile and trying to close on the patrol).

Appendix 2

MEDAL OF HONOR CITATION FOR CPL. DAKOTA L. MEYER, USMC

The President of the United States in the name of The Congress takes pleasure in presenting the **MEDAL OF HONOR** to

CORPORAL DAKOTA L. MEYER
UNITED STATES MARINE CORPS

For service as set forth in the following:

For conspicuous gallantry and intrepidity at the risk of his life above and beyond the call of duty while serving with Marine Embedded Training Team 2–8, Regional Corps Advisory Command 3–7, in Kunar Province, Afghanistan, on 8 September 2009. Corporal Meyer maintained security at a patrol rally point while other members of his team moved on foot with two platoons of Afghan National Army and Border Police into the village of Ganjgal for a pre-dawn meeting with village elders. Moving into the village, the patrol was ambushed by more than 50 enemy fighters firing rocket propelled grenades, mortars, and machine guns from houses and fortified positions on the slopes above. Hearing over the radio that four U.S. team members were cut off, Corporal Meyer seized the initiative. With a fellow Marine driving, Corporal Meyer took the exposed gunner's position in a gun-truck as they drove down the steeply terraced terrain in a daring attempt to disrupt the enemy attack and locate the trapped U.S. team. Disregarding intense enemy fire now concentrated on their lone vehicle, Corporal Meyer killed a number of enemy fighters with the mounted machine guns and his rifle, some at near point blank range, as he and his driver made three solo trips into the ambush area. During the first two trips, he and his driver evacuated two dozen Afghan soldiers, many of whom were wounded. When one machine gun became inoperable, he directed a return to the rally point to switch to another gun-truck for a third trip into the ambush area where his accurate fire directly supported the remaining U.S. personnel and Afghan soldiers fighting their way out of the ambush. Despite a shrapnel wound to his arm, Corporal Meyer made two more trips into the ambush area in a third gun-truck accompanied by four other Afghan vehicles to recover more wounded Afghan soldiers and search for the missing U.S. team members. Still under heavy enemy fire, he dismounted the vehicle on the fifth trip and moved on foot to locate and recover the bodies of his team members. Corporal Meyer's daring initiative and bold fighting spirit throughout the 6-hour battle significantly disrupted the enemy's attack and inspired the members of the combined force to fight on. His unwavering courage and steadfast devotion to his U.S. and Afghan comrades in the face of almost certain death reflected great credit upon himself and upheld the highest traditions of the Marine Corps and the United States Naval Service.

Notes

The Central Command posted online a redacted but full account of the investigation by Cols. Werth and Hooker on November 25, 2009. The citations from the online documents list the exhibits by alphabetical reference; e.g., Exhibit N. The hard copy of the Werth/Hooker account lists the statements by unit and alphanumerically; e.g., Members of 1–32 Task Force Chosin, Exhibit A.1. Wherever possible, I have given both citations.

The sworn statements from the Medal of Honor packets are cited separately by an indication of the alphabetical tab reference for Meyer's packet and the appendix reference for Swenson's packet. All references to exhibits refer to the Werth/Hooker Investigation.

INTRODUCTION: ALONG THE AFGHAN-PAKISTAN BORDER

5 *Staff Sgt. Kenefick and Lt. Johnson:* For the sake of Marine traditions, let me set one thing straight. On our advisor team, I never called my seniors by their first names. That is done in the SEALs and Special Forces teams, but usually not in Marine advisor units. When I write about the lieutenant and the staff sergeant in this book, sometimes I use their first names because the four of us were friends, but each of us knew his position in the chain of command.

7 *Battalion 1–32, tasked with preventing enemy infiltration from Pakistan:* The battalion, called Chosin, was from the 10th Mountain Division and working in Afghanistan as part of a brigade called Task Force Mountain Warrior.

7 *Afghan battalion that we were advising*: At Monti, we were advising the 3rd Coy (Company) of the 2nd Kandak, 215th Corps. The kandak/battalion's headquarters was at Camp Joyce.

8 *"Kunar people like Americans," he told each new team of advisors*: Eshok conversation with West on several occasions, including 17 Oct. 2009 at Joyce.

8 *Joyce would focus on straightening out the screwed-up Afghan logistics*: As Maj. Williams explained at Joyce to West on 17 Oct. 2009, "For instance, we supplied the kandak with plastic water jugs. Now the Afghan S-4 [logistics officer] says they're gone—disappeared—and he wants us to come up with more. No, that's the wrong request. He has money from his own chain of command; he buys replacements or he finds the jugs he lost. I don't have any I'm going to give him."

CHAPTER 1: FINISH THE GAME

26 *"If you make it through, you can become a grunt"*: Every year, between 7 and 10 percent of all recruits drop out of boot camp. Aline O. Quester, *Marine Corps Recruits: A Historical Look at Accessions and Boot Camp Performance* (Alexandria, VA: Center for Naval Analyses, 2010).

CHAPTER 2: THE MARINE YEARS

32 *he killed more than five hundred Russian soldiers*: Tapio A. M. Saarelainen, *The Sniper: Simo Häyhä* (Tampere, Finland: Apali, 2008), 135 pages. (Saarelainen cites a figure of 542; others put it at 505. Several sources agree the number was above 500. Häyhä after the war became a champion moose hunter.)

33 *Chris Kyle, a SEAL, recorded 160 kills*: Chris Kyle, *American Sniper* (New York: Morrow, 2012), p. 5.

CHAPTER 5: COMING TOGETHER

65 *The border meant nothing to the tribes*: Paul Overby, *Holy Blood* (New York: Praeger, 1993), p. 162. Overby described fighting alongside the mujahideen stationed at Dangam in 1988. He had walked across from Pakistan.

CHAPTER 6: OUT OF THE SMOKE

70 *Lt. Johnson calmed down the driver:* Lt. Johnson report, "Report on Rocket Attack at Monti, 6 September 2009." "I left the tower," he wrote, "to coordinate an LTV [a Ford] pickup of the wounded soldier. Once the LTV pulled up to the guard tower, Cpl. Meyer picked up the wounded soldier and under indirect and direct fire carried him down two flights of stairs to the truck."

CHAPTER 7: GANJIGAL

75 *pay for a tribal militia that would stop the rockets:* West notes from meeting with Ganjigal elders, together with Lt. Cols. Ayoub and O'Donnell at ABP base next to FOB Joyce, 9 July 2009.

75 *"They owe you nothing for your bad behavior":* West notes from meeting with Ayoub, Lt. Col. O'Donnell, and the Ganjigal elders, 9 July 2009.

75 *"with zero status inside the village":* Capt. Kaplan conversation with West, 1 Dec. 2011.

75 *"pro-U.S. and supportive of the Afghan government":* Dept. of the Army, AFZC-BCT-AD, 25 Sept. 2009, Subject: AR 15–6 Investigation, Cols. R. D. Hooker, USA, and J. F. Werth, USMC, Exhibit N (E.1).

78 *Taliban had not sprung ambushes from inside villages:* Memo for Record, 25 Nov. 2009, CJTF-82, AR 15–6 Report of Investigation re Operations in the Ganjigal Valley, 8 Sept. 2009.

80 *Gal Rahman, a border police chief:* West conversations with Kerr and Swenson at Joyce and Monti, July and Oct. 2009.

80 *soft American target:* Swenson email to West, April 18, 2012.

81 *"Three-070 is the Undo KE, correct?":* Swenson email to West, 23 Jan. 2012.

81 *"we could put smoke on the deck for screening":* Maj. Castro AR 15–6 Investigation, 21 Sept. 2009, Appendix S.

81 *"KE 3070":* Swenson briefing to Bing West at FOB Joyce, 13 Oct. 2009.

81 *Battalion 1–32 believed Williams was in charge:* Memo for Record, 25 Nov. 2009, CJTF-82, AR 15–6 Report of Investigation re Operations in the Ganjigal Valley, 8 Sept. 2009, Section II: Findings and Recommendations.

81 *Maj. Talib, the operations officer of the Afghan battalion, was in command:*

Memo for Record, 25 Nov. 2009, CJTF-82, AR 15–6 Report of Investigation re Operations in the Ganjigal Valley, 8 Sept. 2009, Section II: Findings and Recommendations.

84 *equipment density list:* Werth/Hooker Investigation, Exhibit BH. Note: Fabayo (BH) and Swenson (BI) gave extensive statements of what happened and what they believed went wrong. Both statements were included in the Werth/Hooker report yet not listed in index.

84–5 *thirty-two fighters were moving from Pakistan to reinforce Ganjigal:* Mirc Chat, 2356 Zulu, Actions in Contact, Appendix c4 of Swenson packet, report from ODA received previously at 1728Z; see also MIRC Chat time, Cpl. Dakota L. Meyer, Medal of Honor packet, Tab C.

85 *two kilometers north of Ganjigal village:* See entries in Meyer packet, Tab C. Also see Mirc Chat, 1909 Zulu, Actions in Contact, Appendix c4. Times for enemy movement are given in Zulu: 1727Z, 1909Z, 1922Z.

85 *Fabayo knew nothing of these movements:* However, Capt. Kaplan later testified that "reporting received and briefed immediately prior to the operation indicated the presence of 45–60 AAF (Anti-Afghan Forces)." Werth/Hooker Investigation, 25 Nov. 2009, Exhibit L (D.1).

85 *"stopping under cover and hesitating at all open areas":* Mirc Chat, 0005 Zulu, Actions in Contact, Appendix c4 (Swenson).

85 *perfect intelligence a day ahead of our movement:* Rahman, a cleric, was the Taliban regional commander for Kunar and two other provinces. He led a hard-core group called JDQ, a branch of Al Qaeda that included Arab fighters and Chechens. See "Syed Saleem Shahzad, a Fighter and a Financier," *Asia Times*, 23 May 2008.

85 *two on the south side, and one in the middle:* Dept. of the Army, Memorandum for the Record, AFZC-BCT-AD, 21 Sept. 2009, Subject: AR 15–6 Investigation, Colonels R. D. Hooker, USA, and J. F. Werth, USMC, Exhibit II-1. To wit: The next afternoon, an informer reported that Taliban commanders Faqir and Ismael had entered Ganjigal on 7 September. An informant inside the Border Police had tipped them off about the Key Leader Engagement mission. A Wikileaks entry from the JTF spot reports re the Ganjigal ambush read as follows: "Already 20 T [Taliban] were in the village. Hanifullah, Haji Mamiran and Niam were the three chief planners. Mamhullah Khadim had 15 Taliban in his group; Zia Ur Rahman had 15. AAF [Anti-Afghan Forces] were staging in Pakistan. Faqir brought

in 20 more and set up in five positions; two on north side and two on south side and one in middle."

85 *two kilometers northeast of Ganjigal:* Mirc Chat, 2343 Zulu, Actions in Contact, Appendix c4 (Swenson).

85 *served as a major supply point in the war against the Russians:* Cols. R. D. Hooker, USA, and J. F. Werth, USMC, Exhibit L (D.1). In his statement, Capt. Kaplan was furious because Ganjigal was never estimated to hold in excess of twenty to thirty military-aged males, yet reporting immediately prior to the battle "indicated 45–60 AAF [anti-Afghan forces]," prepared to ambush CF (coalition forces). Kaplan was not informed of the updates after midnight by the Joyce TOC as he moved to his OP position. The TOC was not keeping Kaplan, the intel officer on the patrol, up to date with the Mirc Chat reports of enemy reinforcements.

CHAPTER 8: INTO THE VALLEY

91 *the house of an imam, one of the village elders:* Fabayo statement, Feb. 2, 2010, DA Form 2823.

91 *They had a dozen fixed positions:* An estimate of the positions plotted in different sworn statements numbered between eight and eleven.

93 *returned fire, killing the enemy gunner:* Werth/Hooker Investigation, Exhibit AC. (Note not listed in the Index of Exhibits.) Statement by Cpl. Norman, 17 Sept. 2009.

93 *Kaplan, and Cpl. Norman would duel with PKM and AK gunners:* Werth/Hooker Investigation, Exhibit L (D.1). Also statements by Kaplan to West.

94 *"Kilo Echo 3070. Will adjust":* See CJTF-82 Memo for Record, Timeline of Events: Ganjigal, 23 Nov. 2009. See, for instance, entries for 0537 and 0546. There is confusion among Mirc Chat, the Werth/Hooker Investigation, and statements of participants about the exact sequence of the fire requests. Regardless of which KE was called first, the results were the same: only a few rounds were fired. According to Werth/Hooker, upon Granger's order, the artillery stopped completely around 0630, to include any rounds intended to obscure the battlefield.

94 *The southern ridgeline was so high that Swenson's radio:* Swenson brief to West at FOB Joyce, 13 Oct. 2011.

CHAPTER 9: PARALYSIS

95 *Valadez, up on the northern ridge—answered on the net:* Rodriguez-Chavez statement, Tab N. (All references to Tabs are found in the Medal of Honor packet of Cpl. Meyer, cited in "Request for Copy of Documents contained in Medal of Honor Recommendation," Military Awards Branch, U.S. Marine Corps, 28 Oct. 2011.)

95 *"Fox 9 says you are to stay at your present location":* Valadez statement, Tab P.

97 *four hundred meters to the east:* Fabayo statement, Appendix e14 of Medal of Honor packet assembled for the recommendation for Capt. William Swenson attached to a Letter of Lateness from USFORA Afghanistan signed by Col. Chevallier, USA, on 11 Aug. 2011.

98 *the enemy's heavy guns were firing:* JTF-82 Memo for Record, Timeline of Events: Ganjigal, 23 Nov. 2009, 0556.

98 *I may not make it out of here:* Swenson extended conversations with West, 14–17 Oct. 2009, at Camp Joyce and while riding around the district.

99 *higher on the ridge, at least seven times:* Werth/Hooker Investigation, Exhibit L (D.1).

101 *"The fucks won't shoot the arty":* Kaplan discussion with West at Joyce, 15–16 Oct. 2009.

101 *Swenson had identified enemy positions at four grid positions:* The grids were 992 521, 983 512, 981 509, and 957 493.

101 *"I'm making the decision, not them":* Swenson conversation with West at Joyce, 15 Oct. 2009.

101 *"KE 3365, Hill 1485":* JTF-82 Memo for Record, Timeline of Events: Ganjigal, 23 Nov. 2009, request at 0556.

102 *called in a polar mission:* Werth/Hooker Investigation, Exhibits AE and AF (Shadow statements).

102 *"hit from the north, east, and south":* Werth/Hooker Investigation, Exhibit K (C.1).

102 *"twenty questions":* Summers Shadow 4 Appendix G6, Werth/Hooker Investigation.

102 *A second string was running the show, and not well:* The leaders in the TOC came from the second tier inside 1–32. The battle captain had been relieved of his platoon before the deployment began. Lt. Col. O'Donnell was

on leave. His executive officer, a major, had a checkered reputation; in previous battles, platoon leaders under fire had decided to ignore his orders over the radio.

102 *no more than four or five effective rounds:* Fabayo, Exhibit BH.

102 *an eight-round "splash"—with shells on target—inside ten minutes:* JTF-82 Memo for Record, Timeline of Events: Ganjigal, 23 Nov. 2009, splash 0605.

102 *fire mission requests were cascading in:* See Fabayo, Appendix e11, Garza, Appendix e15, and CJTF-82 Timeline.

102 *every four minutes:* Mirc CHAT fire mission requests were logged in at 0537, 0541, 0546, 0550, 0556, and 0600.

102 *Joyce allowed only twenty-one artillery shells to be fired:* Werth/Hooker Investigation summary (four 155 shells, thirteen 120 shells, and five 120 WP shells).

103 *"the next higher headquarters commander has approved":* ISAF Tactical Directive, 1 July 2009, p. 2.

103 *"disposition of civilians in the area":* Werth/Hooker Investigation, Exhibit T.

104 *Shadow 4 relayed the message to Joyce:* CJTF-82 Memo for Record, Timeline of Events: Ganjigal, 23 Nov. 2009, 0550.

104 *Sgt. Summers kept requesting air:* Werth/Hooker Investigation, Exhibit AF. Summers statement.

104 *Everyone was trying to talk to him, asking for guidance:* Gunny Miller, JP Exhibit V. (The exhibit number was typed at the bottom of the page; it does not appear in the index.)

104 *last four Social Security digits of each American in the valley:* Summers, Appendix G6.

104 *This had to be KE 3070:* CJTF-82, MFR Timeline of Events, 23 Nov. 2009 (0600 entry: four HE 155mm fires splashed on KE 3070).

105 *"We have to get out of here":* Rodriguez-Chavez, Tab N.

CHAPTER 10: LOST

106 *The fight had been raging for over half an hour:* Meyer on CBS interview, *60 Minutes.*

106 *Fabayo told Valadez to stay off the net:* Valadez statement, Tab P.

106 *"You're supposed to stay where you are":* Valadez statement, Tab P.

107 *urging them in Pashto to follow me:* Valadez statement, Tab P.

109 *"you have enemy at your nine o'clock, driver's side":* Miller, Annex E, Appendix e18.

110 *I could get at them easier in the fight ahead:* Rodriguez-Chavez, Tab N.

110 *"There are people out there dying":* Valadez statement, Tab P.

111 *it would arrive in "fifteen mikes":* Fabayo, Appendix e14.

111 *called the ops center at Jalalabad Air Base:* Staff Sgt. Lantz called directly to the ops center of the 7th Squadron, 17th Cavalry Regiment at JAL. The problem was that 7–17 wanted clearance from the brigade level.

111 *The squadron ops chief agreed to re-task the birds immediately:* AR 15–16, Werth/Hooker Investigation, 25 Nov. 2009, Exhibit BJ.

111 *close air support in addition to helicopters:* Werth/Hooker Investigation, 25 Nov. 2009, Exhibit II-1 (P.6). (The TOC could get CAS by declaring an air TIC [Troops In Contact].)

111 *another mission north of Ganjigal was of "higher priority":* AR 15–16, Werth/Hooker Investigation, 25 Nov. 2009, Exhibit C1 and Exhibit R ("The ANA and ABP leadership knew that they would have no CCA") and Exhibit U ("The air is engaged in another mission").

111 *shouting that Ganjigal was "a heavy TIC":* AR 15–16, Werth/Hooker Investigation, 25 Nov. 2009, Exhibits AE and AF and MFR stating conclusions.

111 *Captain Harting ignored Shadow's plea:* AR 15–16, Werth/Hooker Investigation, 25 Nov. 2009. See Exhibit K for the rationale by the battle captain in TOC.

112 *"They said it was unavailable":* Fabayo, Exhibit BH.

112 *laughing at how ridiculous the situation was:* Miller, Annex E, Appendix e18.

112 *"thirty to sixty AAF" (Anti-Afghan Forces) were attacking:* Harting, Exhibit K.

112 *"denied twice due to proximity of structures":* Werth/Hooker Investigation, JP Exhibit K.

112 *wouldn't authorize fire support:* Werth Investigation, Exhibit II-1 (P. 5) ("complete absence of fires from 0639 to 1615").

112 *Swenson and Fabayo sat stunned:* Fabayo, Werth/Hooker Investigation, Exhibit BH.

112 *Lt. Johnson again contacted Fabayo on the radio:* Fabayo, Appendix e14.

112 *"Get us smoke to get us out of here":* Miller, Annex E, Appendix e18.

113 *the village was too close:* Fabayo, Appendix e14.

113 *"They didn't have SA [situational awareness]":* Granger discussion with West at Joyce, 17 Oct. 2009.

114 *"verified that no civilians are present":* Tactical Directive, Headquarters International Security Assistance Force, Kabul, 1 July 2009.

114 *"a potential QRF [quick-reaction force]":* CJTF-82 Memo for Record, Timeline of Events: Ganjigal, 23 Nov. 2009, 0615.

114 *he hadn't been told how far he was to advance:* CJTF-82 Memo for Record, Timeline of Events: Ganjigal, 23 Nov. 2009, 0630.

114 *Maj. Williams handed his cell phone:* Fabayo, Appendix e14.

114 *asking him to call for an Afghan quick-reaction force:* Fabayo, Appendix e11.

114 *without any Americans from 1–32 joining them:* Fabayo, Exhibit BH.

115 *no effect on the enemy rate of fire:* Garza statements, Annex E, Appendix e15, and telephonic interview 16 Sept. 2009, Annex E, Appendix e5.

115 *from the ridges to the south, and from the terraces to the north:* Swenson brief to West, 13 Oct. 2009.

115 *requesting smoke "to conceal their movement":* Fabayo, Appendix e14.

116 *The angle of the fire had shifted southeast:* Fabayo, Appendix e11, 26 Feb. 2010.

116 *more men were shooting at him from inside the town:* Fabayo, Exhibit BH.

116 *A woman in a red and purple dress:* Werth/Hooker Investigation, Exhibit G.

116 *another woman stacking rocks to make fighting position:* Fabayo, Exhibit BH.

116 *the far ambush was becoming a near ambush:* Fabayo, Exhibit BH. "Our far ambush became a near ambush," Fabayo said. "They start to maneuver around us, while we try to withdraw."

117 *an RPG exploded near him, throwing him to the ground:* Garza statement, Annex E, Appendix e5, 16 Sept. 2009, MFR, AFZC-BCT-AD, Maj. Johannes Castro, USA.

117 *ordered the Army platoon—Dog 3–2—to move forward:* 15-6 Investigation, JP Exhibit F and Exhibit K, and Enemy Action Attack RPT Afghan war diary, 2009–09–08 ref. AFG20090908n2165.

117 *"We're surrounded":* Meyer, Annex E, Appendix e3.

118 *Lt. Fabayo saw our Humvee:* Fabayo, Appendix e14.

118 *"You got to keep calm":* Fabayo, Exhibit BH.

118 *"You must surrender"*: Swenson email to West, 5 Jan. 2011.

119 *I don't want some kid to find it intact and blow himself up*: Swenson discussion with West, 14 Sept. 2011.

119 *"Where's the reporter?"*: Fabayo, Exhibit BH.

119 *was dead*: Swenson discussions with West, 17 Oct. 2009 and 14 Sept. 2011.

119 *Swenson, who carried five hundred rounds for his M4*: Swenson discussions with West, 14 Sept. 2011.

119 *the notepad in his pocket had crumbled*: Fabayo, Appendix e12 (Swenson).

119 *handed them anti-infection pills*: Fabayo, Annex E, Appendix e11, and Exhibit BH.

120 *"You'll get shot"*: Garza statement, Appendix e15.

120 *see one Askar stand up and take a bullet in the neck*: Memo for the Record, CJTF-1-CJ1, Transcribed Sworn Statement of CPT Swenson, William D., 29 July 2011.

120 *Fabayo dropped his first-aid bag*: Fabayo, Annex E, Appendix e11.

120 *two OH-58 Kiowas were en route to the valley*: According to Memo for Record, JTF-82, 23 Nov. 2009, Timeline of Events Ganjigal Valley, 7–8 Sept. 2009, at 0720 the SWT Kiowas were wings up from FOB Fenty and they arrived on station at 0745; the official timeline is clear, but unofficially a Marine UAH, according to Swenson (Tab J), diverted without informing higher headquarters and provided initial gun runs around 0715.

121 *he called for a medevac*: Recorded in TOC at Joyce at 0738, Exhibit K.

121 *"Is he Army or Marine?"*: Werth/Hooker Investigation, Gunny Miller, Exhibit U.

121 *grenades impacted behind them and to their right side*: Fabayo, Annex E, Appendix e14.

CHAPTER 11: INTO THE FIRE

123 *Lt. Johnson said he'd cover Hafez*: Werth/Hooker Investigation, Exhibit AJ.

123 *He didn't see or hear Lt. Johnson after that*: telecommunication West and Meyer et al. at Random House with Hafez on 11 Feb. 2012.

124 *Hafez clawed at his gear and threw a smoke grenade*: telecommunication West and Meyer et al. at Random House with Hafez on 11 Feb. 2012.

125 *give a grid. Nine seven*: Meyer, CBS interview, *60 Minutes*.

125 *Valadez came up on the net*: Rodriguez-Chavez statement, Tab N.

125 *"There are a lot of bad guys on both sides"*: Valadez statement, Tab P.

128 *suffered only mild bruises*: Werth/Hooker Investigation, Exhibits AD and AB.

131 *crouched alongside a drainage ditch, not ten meters away*: Meyer After Action Report for Ganjigal, 11 Sept. 2009.

132 *"The gun won't go down enough"*: Statement of Rodriguez-Chavez, Tab O.

132 *"expertise-induced amnesia"*: Jeff Wise, *Extreme Fear* (New York: St. Martin's Press, 2009), p. 50.

132 *the others ducked back into the ditch*: Meyer brief to West at Monti, 17 Oct. 2009. (The notes read that Meyer said he "hit four.")

132 *firing an AK at us from his hip*: Rodriguez-Chavez description to West, teleconference, 31 Jan. 2012.

135 *the pilots couldn't do enough to help us*: Tab R. The first flight of pilots to arrive were CW2 Kristopher Bassett, CW2 James O'Neal, CW2 Ryan Neal, and CW2 Michael McClain.

136 *ignoring the RPG shells exploding in the air*: CWO Silano description to West, telecommunication, 3 June 2012.

CHAPTER 12: INTO THE WASH

138 *six Afghan soldiers were dead and nine wounded*: Werth/Hooker Investigation, 25 Nov. 2009, Exhibit II-1 (P.7).

138 *Swenson brought back two dead jihadists, too*: Swenson, Exhibit BI.

142 *Fabayo got into our turret and Hafez got on the radio*: Fabayo, Annex E, Appendix e12.

146 *picked up Dodd Ali, and rolled his stiff body into the open back*: Swenson wrote to me on 6 Jan. 2012: "At the time, Dakota was a Marine E-4; I did not know him. I was situationally aware of the location of those who fought at the battle, but putting a name to the role performed is different. You referenced football: I know where the QB [quarterback] was, but I do not necessarily recall his roster number. What I witnessed of Dakota's heroism, I am certain of."

CHAPTER 13: PRIMAL

147 *Swenson got out to talk to the Army platoon leader:* Swenson, Tab J.

147 *four Americans were missing:* Werth/Hooker Investigation, Exhibit BR.

148 *"You're not going back into the fight":* Meyer interview with CBS, *60 Minutes.*

148 *left the battlefield:* Werth/Hooker Investigation, Exhibit II-1 (P.7), concluded that "the 2–8 ETT commander, the record shows that he performed capably and courageously."

149 *"Hold where you are":* Silano telecommunication with West, 7 June 2012.

149 *move into the valley:* Email Swenson to West, 6 Jan. 2011.

150 *"Spot":* Meyer interview with CBS, *60 Minutes.*

151 *we pulled out about ten or twelve wounded:* Werth/Hooker Investigation, Exhibit AJ.

152 *waiting their turn to enter the valley:* Bassett statement, Appendix e13, 14 Sept. 2009.

152 *fire missions kept getting denied:* Werth/Hooker Investigation, Exhibit U. "I heard constant requests for fire support," Sgt. Summers, up at Shadow 4, said.

152 *fended off the endless questions from the TOC at Joyce:* Summers, Werth/Hooker Investigation, Exhibit C1, 17 Nov. 2009. "My feeling is that the Marines and Afghan forces were left out to dry," Shadow 4—Sgt. Summers—said. "It's a horrible feeling but that's how I feel about it. QRF? Air? Nothing but endless questions [by the TOC]."

152 *the pilots didn't return fire:* Silano telecommunication with West, 7 June 2012.

153 *they were fighting the outsiders:* This is unsurprising. See, for instance, Olaf Caroe, *The Pathans* (New York: Oxford University Press, 1958), p. 437.

CHAPTER 14: TEAM MONTI

156 *a PKM was still shooting at some Askars:* Fabayo, Appendix e14.

157 *fell into a deep, well-constructed trench:* Swenson brief to West at FOB Joyce, 13 Oct. 2009.

159 *villagers returning to Ganjigal:* The Werth/Hooker investigation (JP, Exhibit A, Part 2, page 16) stated that "no Afghan civilians were either killed

or injured during this operation." In all due respect, this cannot be confirmed. Tens of thousands of bullets were fired over the course of the day. No one walked around keeping count of who was struck, whether Afghan soldiers, civilians who were not involved, civilians who were aiding the enemy, or enemy who were wearing civilian clothes.

CHAPTER 15: DAB KHAR

162 *set the two dead aside for burial:* Exhibits AI and J.
166 *bloody handprints:* Kerr reminded me of this in an email dated July 11, 2012.

CHAPTER 16: CHEERLEADERS

177 *his command had made progress in eastern Afghanistan:* DoD press briefing by Maj. Gen. Scaparrotti, 3 June 2010.
177 *The Americans handed out Korans and prayer rugs:* Regional Command East archives, 19 Dec. 2009, reprint of 3 Dec. 2009 story citing Capt. J. L. Saxe, 1–32.

POSTSCRIPT: SWENSON

193 *"I am staring at the target":* Swenson, Appendix B1.
194 *"I expect to be kicked out":* Swenson to West at Joyce, 18 Oct. 2009.
194 *recommendation for the Medal of Honor in December of 2009:* USFOR-A DCDR-COS Letter of Lateness: Medal of Honor Recommendation, Captain William D. Swenson, United States Army, signed by Col. J. H. Chevallier, USA, 11 Aug. 2011. (Swenson was part of a sixteen-man team advising seven Afghan Border Police units along a 480-kilometer stretch of the Afghanistan/Pakistan border. There was very little internal administrative support for the police advisor program. For fitness reports and ratings, Swenson was evaluated by Battalion 1–32 at Camp Joyce.)
194 *commanded by Maj. Gen. Curtis Scaparrotti:* USFOR-A DCDR-COS Letter of Lateness: Medal of Honor Recommendation, Captain William D. Swenson, United States Army, signed by Col. J. H. Chevallier, USA, 11 Aug. 2011.

194 *signatures required for the Medal of Honor:* Army Regulation 600–8-22, 15 Sept. 2011.

194 *one of the most important things a commander does in combat:* Michelle Tan, "Missing Medals," *Army Times*, 2 June 2012.

195 *investigation by the television correspondent Dan Rather: Dan Rather Reports*, TV series, 13 Sept. 2011.

195 *packet recommending the Medal of Honor:* The narrative written to justify the recommendation for Swenson's Medal of Honor implied, despite Swenson's testimony, that strong artillery support had been provided at Ganjigal. "Due to the extreme close proximity of insurgent fighters to their ANSF [Afghan National Security Forces] positions," the narrative stated, "multiple fire missions were unsuccessful in deterring the enemy's advance." Source: Narrative for the Medal of Honor, Cpt. William D. Swenson, undated, p. 3.

195 *guidelines were crystal-clear, with no ambiguity:* See Army Regulation 600–8-22.

195 *uploaded into the Army electronic archives:* AR 600–8-22 Military Awards, Fort Knox, KY, plus DA form 638.

196 *Army Sgt. 1st Class Westbrook:* Although his bravery went without official recognition, the Marines deeply appreciated his devotion to his comrades. Mr. Punch Haynes of the Marine Corps—Law Enforcement Foundation donated a series of $30,000 scholarships to the Westbrook children in appreciation for Sgt. Westbrook's stand beside his fellow Marines.

196 *informed the Marine Central Command about the recommendation for Swenson:* Col. Yoo memos to MarCentCom, on 5 and 10 Aug. 2010.

196 *he was noting this "for the record":* Col. Daniel D. Yoo to MarCentCom, response to request for information, 5 Aug. 2010.

196 *"This has caused disquiet among those who were at Ganjigal":* West email to Gen. Casey, 19 April 2011.

196 *found the lost recommendation, and resubmitted it in August:* USFOR-A DDR-COS, 11 Aug. 2011.

196 *"Because it was the right thing to do":* Bing West, "The Afghan Rescue Mission Behind Today's Medal of Honor," *Wall Street Journal*, 15 Sept. 2011.

196 *"Be the hunter": Washington Post*, 9 July 2010. "You go into Afghanistan," Mattis said, "you got guys who slap women around for five years, because they didn't wear a veil. You know guys like that ain't got no manhood left anyway. So it's a hell of a lot of fun to shoot 'em."

197 *Lute had the reputation of being a straight shooter:* Meyer sent the email on 30 Nov. 2011.

200 *Every retelling of battle is a description of confusion:* Researchers have estimated that 37 percent of the memory about details of a chaotic event has changed a year after the event. See William Hirst, Elizabeth A. Phelps, et al., "Long-Term Memory for the Terrorist Attack of September 11: Flashbulb Memories, Event Memories, and the Factors That Influence Their Retention," *Journal of Experimental Psychology*, American Psychological Association, 2009.

201 *No outpost was ever established in the valley of Ganjigal:* Email from Sgt. Eric Jones, 1–235 INF, to West, 17 Apr. 2012.

201 *a hard-core Islamist dedicated to winning:* QZR kidnapped the British aid worker Linda Norgrove, who was killed in a rescue attempt in October of 2010.

201 *"positively identified enemy forces within a residential compound":* Headquarters, International Security Assistance Force, Tactical Directive, Kabul, 1 July 2009.

202 *"situations in which there may be no non-hostile actors":* Werth/Hooker Investigation, Exhibit L.

202 *"you always have the right to defend yourself":* Fabayo, Annex E, Appendix e12.

203 *"you'll not be forgotten":* Maj. Gen. Curtis Scaparrotti, USA, DoD News Transcript, 3 June 2010.

203 *cover-up for the higher-ups:* Dan Herbeck, "Marine's Death Stirs Cover-up Questions," *Buffalo News*, Dec. 11, 2011.

203 *"it's going to save lives":* Werth/Hooker Investigation, Exhibit BI.

203 *"The key here is to empower and not be the bottleneck":* Orin Harari, *The Leadership Secrets of Colin Powell* (New York: McGraw-Hill, 2002).

204 *Rodriguez-Chavez several times thought he had been killed:* Rodriguez-Chavez remark to West, 22 April 2012.

204 *Fabayo tried to wave off the chopper:* Fabayo, Exhibit BH.

DAKOTA MEYER was born and raised in Columbia, Kentucky, and enlisted in the United States Marine Corps in 2006. A school-trained sniper and highly skilled infantryman, Cpl. Meyer deployed to Iraq in 2007 and to Afghanistan in 2009. In 2011, he was awarded the Congressional Medal of Honor for his unyielding courage in the battle of Ganjigal. He now competes at charity events in skeet and rifle competitions. He also speaks frequently at schools and veterans' events to raise awareness of our military and remains dedicated to the causes of our veterans. For the families of wounded troops, he has raised more than one million dollars.

www.dakotameyer.com

BING WEST, a Marine combat veteran, served as an assistant secretary of defense in the Reagan administration. He has been on hundreds of patrols in Vietnam, Iraq, and Afghanistan. A nationally acclaimed war correspondent, he is the author of *The Village, No True Glory, The Strongest Tribe,* and *The Wrong War.* A member of the Council on Foreign Relations, West has received the Marine Corps Heritage Foundation award for nonfiction, the Colby Award for military nonfiction, the Veterans of Foreign Wars News Media Award, and the Marine Corps University Foundation's Russell Leadership Award. He lives with his wife, Betsy, in Newport, Rhode Island.

westwrite.com